LEARNING FOR LIFE AND WORK 3

NI Key Stage 3

P. Dornan, K. Armstrong,
L. Curragh, J. McCusker,
L. McEvoy, P. Smith

HODDER EDUCATION
AN HACHETTE UK COMPANY

The Publishers would like to thank the following for permission to reproduce copyright material:

Photo credits

p.8 © Galina Barskaya/Fotolia; **p.14** © Rémi Cauzid/Fotolia; **p.16** © picsfive/Fotolia; **p.17** © Frederic Haslin/TempSport/Corbis; **p.20** *CL* © Eric Nathan/Alamy; *BL* © Les Gibbon/Alamy; **p.21** © Ian Shaw/Alamy; **p.22** *CL* © Herjua; *CR* © Sander Van de Wijngaert; **p.23** *L–R* © Adrian Sherratt/Alamy; © David Levenson/Alamy; © Sally and Richard Greenhill/Alamy; © Jon Feingersh/zefa/Corbis; **p.24** © Elena Korenbaum; **p.25** © Elena Elisseeva/Fotolia; **p.26** © Peter Arnold, Inc./Alamy; **p.28** *TL* © Christine Osborne Pictures/Alamy; *CL* © Rich Vintage; **p.30** © Bubbles Photolibrary/Alamy; **p.31** © Asiseeit; **p.33** *TL* © Tomasz Szymanski/Fotolia; *TM* © Luoman; *TR* © Mark Sykes/Alamy; *CL* © Edyta Pawlowska/Fotolia; *CM* © Tal Delbari; **p.36** Courtesy of Lesley McEvoy; **p.39** *T–B* © Thomas Sztanek/Fotolia; © Chris Schmidt; © Galina Barskaya/Fotolia; © Jim West/Alamy; **p.42** *CL* © Robert Kelly/Fotolia; *BL* © Paul Cummings/Fotolia; *BM* © Jenny/Fotolia; *BR* © Sébastien Maurer/Fotolia; **p.43** Logo courtesy of Northern Ireland Assembly; **p.46** Logo courtesy of Oxfam; **51** *TR* © Lyndon Giffard/Alamy; *CL–R* © Jeff Widener/AP/PA Photos; cartoon © David Brown/ Cartoonstock; © maggiegowan.co.uk/Alamy; **p.52** *L–R* © Paul Doyle/Alamy; © Les Gibbon/Alamy; © Robert Hollingworth/Alamy; © William Meyer/Alamy; **p.54** *T–B* © Stephen Finn/Fotolia; © JoeFox/Alamy; © Broker/Fotolia; © Larry Lilac/Alamy; © Paul Murphy/Fotolia; © Picture Art/Fotolia; © Jenny/Fotolia; © Stephen VanHorn/Fotolia; © Edi/Fotolia; © Ernest Prim/Fotolia; **p.60** *L–R* © Photo Researchers/Alamy; Courtesy of NICEM; ATD Fourth World; Courtesy of Lesley McEvoy; **p.65** *T* © Nick Gregory/ Alamy; *C* © Daniel Heighton/Alamy; **p.66** © Leah-Anne Thompson/Istock; **p.72** *TL* © Andrew Holt/Alamy; *CL* © Jacom Stephens/ Istock; *CM* © visi.stock/Fotolia; *CR* © Inna Felker/Fotolia; *BL* © Eliza Snow; *BM* © Deanm/Fotolia; *BR* © AA World Travel Library/ Alamy; **p.78** © tompiodesign.com/Alamy; **p.79** © Ian Shaw/Alamy; **p.81** © PB/Fotolia; **p.82** *T–B* © Libby Welch/Alamy; © Leah-Anne Thompson/Fotolia; © BITC/SuperValu; **p.86** © Barbara P. Fernandez/Corbis; **p.87** © JUPITERIMAGES/ Comstock Premium/Alamy; **p.88** *L–R* © Fotolia IX/Fotolia; © Alexander Rochau/Fotolia; © Frank van Haalen.

Acknowledgements

p.73 The Northern Ireland Fire and Rescue Service for the questionnaire 'A Day in the Life … Firefighter'; **p.80** Students Partnership Worldwide for the 'Ellie Messham' case study; Real Gap Year Experience for the 'Lucy Feltham' case study; **p.82** Belfast telegraph for the article 'Adopt a school is teaching all a valuable lesson'; Business in the Community/SuperValu for the article and photograph 'Supervalu helps charity get BIG BUS on the road'; **p.86** Business Link for the 'entrepreneurial quality check' data

Every effort has been made to trace all copyright holders, but if any have been inadvertently overlooked the Publishers will be pleased to make the necessary arrangements at the first opportunity.

Although every effort has been made to ensure that website addresses are correct at time of going to press, Hodder Education cannot be held responsible for the content of any website mentioned in this book. It is sometimes possible to find a relocated web page by typing in the address of the home page for a website in the URL window of your browser.

Hachette UK's policy is to use papers that are natural, renewable and recyclable products and made from wood grown in sustainable forests. The logging and manufacturing processes are expected to conform to the environmental regulations of the country of origin.

Orders: please contact Bookpoint Ltd, 130 Milton Park, Abingdon, Oxon OX14 4SB. Telephone: (44) 01235 827720. Fax: (44) 01235 400454. Lines are open 9.00–5.00, Monday to Saturday, with a 24-hour message answering service. Visit our website at www.hoddereducation.co.uk

© Peter Dornan, Kathryn Armstrong, Lois Curragh, John McCusker, Lesley McEvoy and Paula Smith 2009

First published in 2009 by

Hodder Education,

An Hachette UK Company

338 Euston Road

London NW1 3BH

Impression number   5 4 3 2

Year   2013 2012 2011 2010 2009

All rights reserved. Apart from any use permitted under UK copyright law, no part of this publication may be reproduced or transmitted in any form or by any means, electronic or mechanical, including photocopying and recording, or held within any information storage and retrieval system, without permission in writing from the publisher or under licence from the Copyright Licensing Agency Limited. Further details of such licences (for reprographic reproduction) may be obtained from the Copyright Licensing Agency Limited, Saffron House, 6–10 Kirby Street, London EC1N 8TS.

Cover photos: *St George's Market*, © Richard Wayman/Alamy; *left to right*, © Digital Vision/Photolibrary Group, © Bruno Vincent/Getty Images, © David Epperson/Photographer's Choice/Photolibrary Group.

Illustrations by GreenGate Publishing Services, Alex Machin and Barry Glennard

Typeset in New Century Schoolbook 11pt by GreenGate Publishing Services, Tonbridge, Kent

Printed in Italy

A catalogue record for this title is available from the British Library.

ISBN: 978 0340 927 106

CONTENTS

Introduction — 1

Personal Development

1. How can I be a person of integrity? — 2
2. How can I develop as a spiritual person? — 4
3. How do I accept 'personal responsibility' in my life? — 6
4. How do I manage impulses? — 8
5. How can I become better at planning? — 10
6. How do I think critically? — 12
7. How do I develop refusal skills? — 14
8. How do I motivate myself? — 16
9. How do I manage personal change? — 18
10. What risk does alcohol present for teenagers? — 20
11. What's the difference between being male and female? — 22
12. How do I deal with loneliness? — 24
13. What are the pros and cons of using contraception? — 26
14. How do I avoid sexually transmitted infections? — 28
15. Where can I get help in my community? — 30

Local and Global Citizenship

16. What do we mean by democracy? — 32
17. Is 'participation' a human right? — 34
18. Do children have a right to participate? — 36
19. How can I participate in my school? — 38
20. How can people actively participate in their society? — 40
21. Who makes the decisions that affect me? — 42
22. What decisions can my representatives make? — 44

23	Why should I take action in a democracy?	46
24	How can we carry out an action project?	48
25	What are the characteristics of democracy?	50
26	What is the role of human rights in a democracy?	52
27	Why do we need laws in a democracy?	54
28	How do breaches of the law affect the community?	56
29	How can laws be enforced?	58
30	What have I learned about citizenship?	60

Education for Employability

31	How do I make decisions?	62
32	Where can I get help?	64
33	How do I start to choose a career?	66
34	What are my 'options'?	68
35	Which subjects should I study?	70
36	What types of jobs are in demand?	72
37	What do people gain from work?	74
38	How can I make myself more employable?	76
39	Can I work in Europe?	78
40	Where in the world can I work?	80
41	Can I make a difference by working in business?	82
42	Can I work for myself?	84
43	Could I start a business?	86

Answers	90
Index	91

INTRODUCTION

Hello and welcome! *Learning for Life and Work*'s aim is to help you to achieve your potential and to make informed and responsible decisions throughout your life journey of growth and change. The purpose is to help you develop:

1 as an individual (mostly but not only through Personal Development),
2 as a contributor to society (mostly through Local and Global Citizenship),
3 as a contributor to the economy and environment (mostly through Education for Employability).

Each book in the course is divided into these three main sections and then broken down into topics. Each topic has a big question as its title to investigate. Throughout the topics you will find the following features.

Learning intentions

Each topic starts by outlining the learning intentions – these are the skills and knowledge you should be learning as you make your way through the topic.

Activities

Each topic has a number of activities. You may be asked to work as an individual, in pairs, in small groups or as a class. The activities have a structure, but because each person and group is unique, there is room for you to be unpredictable and come up with something that no one else has thought of. The activities work best when you are enthusiastic, give them a go and develop and agree some helpful ground rules for working with others. Have fun!

Thinking skills and personal capabilities

Alongside each activity there is an icon. There are five different icons in all and these signpost the main thinking skills and personal capabilities you will be developing while carrying out the activity. The following table shows which skills each icon stands for.

Skill	Icon	Description
Managing Information		Research and manage information effectively to investigate personal development, citizenship and employability issues.
Thinking, Problem Solving, Decision Making		Show deeper understanding by thinking critically and flexibly, solving problems and making informed decisions.
Being Creative		Demonstrate creativity and initiative when developing ideas and following them through.
Working with Others		Work effectively with others.
Self-Management		Demonstrate self-management by working systematically, persisting with tasks, evaluating and improving own performance.

Personal journal

Some activities are designed to encourage you to keep a personal journal. This will help you understand three key questions:

1 Where have I been?
2 Where am I now?
3 Where do I want to go?

Personal journals will help you make sense of your journey and are a particularly useful tool to help assessment. This means your personal journal may be seen by your teacher, family or classmates. It may be personal but it won't be private!

1 HOW CAN I BE A PERSON OF INTEGRITY?

Learning intentions

I am learning:
- ✓ what being a person of integrity means
- ✓ to develop a more consistent level of integrity.

Life worth living doesn't happen by accident. It takes hard work, thought and planning to become a person of integrity. Integrity is about a person's character and involves two key things:

1) All the parts of me fit together, pulling in the same direction to create a life that works and makes sense. I practise what I preach.
2) The outcome of integrity is good and blesses me and others who meet me.

In the following activities you will explore these two themes and then measure how much integrity means to us and our lifestyle.

Activity 1 Defining and exploring integrity

In groups:
Discuss together whether it is possible to have integrity and then:

- say that you respect someone and steal from them?
- believe that all people are created equal, except for men, who are inferior to women?
- hate someone in your heart, but act kindly towards them in practice?
- claim to value yourself, but poison your body with alcohol by getting drunk?
- claim that Hitler was a person of integrity because he practised what he preached?

Activity 2 The results of integrity and duplicity

All actions have consequences. Consider how the things you do can affect parts of your whole self in different ways. Think carefully and then copy and complete the table below to show the consequences of being a person of integrity or a person with double standards. It may help to think in terms of opposites. The examples will help you get started.

	A person of integrity	A person with double standards
Physical body	Healthy eating	
Thoughts		
Feelings	At peace	
Relationships		
Conscience		
Beliefs		Hypocrite
Environment	Recycle and reuse	

Personal Development

Activity 3 How much integrity do I have?

In groups:
Think through the following situations and work out what you would do in each case. First of all, outline your beliefs and values about the situation, then say what you would do. Reflect on how well your beliefs and actions match up and whether the results are good for you and others.

a) In form class you find a £10 note on the floor. What do you believe about stealing? What would you say about it or do with the £10? If you found an MP3 player, would you behave in the same way? Why or why not?

b) In Personal Development class, you have had a lot of discussion about romantic relationships and the need for mutual respect. Your friend is having difficulty in their relationship and wants to end it. They ask you if they could dump their partner respectfully by text. What would you say?

c) Your favourite band's new album has just been released. Trouble is, you are broke! Your friend gives you a web address where you can download it free. What would you do and why?

d) Your Geography coursework is due tomorrow. In your research you find a project online that matches what you have to do perfectly. Do you use it or not?

Activity 4 Personal journal

a) Consider your answers in Activity 3. Do you think they provide the evidence to show that you are a person of integrity? Are you consistent in terms of character? What have you learned about yourself?

b) How important is integrity to you?

c) What could you do yourself or with others to develop your integrity?

2 | HOW CAN I DEVELOP AS A SPIRITUAL PERSON?

Learning intentions

I am learning:
- what spirituality means
- to identify my spiritual qualities and resources
- what my spiritual worldview is.

Have you ever wondered about the meaning of life, the universe and everything? Why are we here and what is the point of it all? We are organisms that can see, hear, taste, touch and smell, but there is 'more' to human beings than just a collection of material atoms and chemicals. The part of us that relates to our non-physical being is called our 'spirit'. People who understand and can connect with what is beyond the physical and material are said to be spiritual.

Activity 1 — Identifying spiritual assets

In groups:

a) Discuss the words in the table. Which are spiritual qualities and resources? Can you think of other spiritual qualities?

b) Make a list of the concepts that are important to you and of the spiritual characteristics and resources you have.

Faith	Hope	Love	Trust
Calling	Gifted	Humility	Vision
Positive in difficulty	Choice	Freedom/Free will	Superstition
Meaning	Purpose	God	Integrity
Suffering	Self-sacrifice	Mercy	Justice
Honesty	Worship	Risk	Awe
Wonder	Relationship	Compassion	Ritual
Tradition	Doctrine	Truth	Authority
Creativity	Peace	Respect	Other?

What is a spiritual worldview?

Every human being has a worldview. A worldview is the framework of ideas and beliefs through which an individual interprets the world and interacts with it.

Different cultures and religions create their own spiritual worldviews. The diagram below shows the physical world and the spiritual world beyond the physical. Your spiritual worldview allows you to see, connect with, or ignore these worlds. To discover your spiritual worldview, you need to identify three key elements: your spiritual knowledge, beliefs and practices. In Activity 2 you will quickly sketch out a rough map of your own spiritual ways of seeing and knowing.

SPIRITUAL WORLD — The world beyond with God(s) and spiritual forces | Religion

Interaction between supernatural and natural forces

PHYSICAL WORLD — Material world of the senses | Science

Personal Development

4

Activity 2   Mapping my spiritual worldview

In pairs:
Each answer these questions and make very brief notes about what you think, believe and do. Explain your spiritual worldview to your partner.

START

Spiritual knowledge
a) Do you believe that there is anything beyond time and space, i.e. things that are eternal?
b) Do you believe in a God or gods that have a greater reality and power than yourself?
- There is one God = monotheism (Christianity, Judaism, Islam).
- There is no God (Buddhism, Humanism, Atheism), or no God that I can find yet (Agnosticism).
- There are many gods (Pantheism, Hinduism).
- All is God (New Age).

c) Do you believe in an organised religion? Why? Do you participate in any religious traditions, rituals or acts of worship?
d) What is the main belief system of your family and the culture you identify with? Do you agree with that belief system?

Spiritual beliefs
a) Is life just an accident, or do things happen for a reason as part of a bigger plan?
b) Do you have faith or hope in anything? If so, what?
c) Can you be spiritual and not religious? Are you religious or spiritual, both or neither?
d) How do you deal with evil, pain, suffering or adversity in your life? Who do you turn to? How do you make sense of it?
e) Why are you here on Earth? What is your unique contribution? Do you have a sense of purpose for your life?

Spiritual practice
a) Do you ever find yourself praying (particularly when you are in difficulty)? If so, to whom and for what?
b) Whom or what do you worship?
- What do you treasure most or spend most of your free time doing?
- Whom do you give the main control of your life over to? Are **you** in charge; are **other people** in charge of you; or do you give charge of your life over to **God(s)**?

c) What traditions or rituals do you follow (including superstitions, habits, holidays, family)?

FINISH

Activity 3   Personal journal

Do you consider yourself a spiritual person?

Personal Development

3 HOW DO I ACCEPT 'PERSONAL RESPONSIBILITY' IN MY LIFE?

> **Learning intentions**
> *I am learning:*
> ✓ the meaning of personal responsibility
> ✓ how to determine appropriate levels of responsibility.

When you take personal responsibility for something, it means that you are going to take appropriate steps towards a situation or action, do something about it and accept whatever the outcome is. Accepting responsibility means not expecting someone else to act on your behalf, facing up to the consequences of an action and responding in whatever way is required. The diagram below shows the steps in taking personal responsibility for something.

THE PROCESS

1 Assess
Identifying the situation:
- What is the situation?
- Are there multiple causes?
- Can I influence the source of this issue directly or indirectly?

2 Determine
Assigning and owning responsibility:
- Is the situation my responsibility?
- What actions could I take?
- Which is the most appropriate action?

3 React
Forming a plan to take appropriate action:
- I am going to continue …
- I am going to stop …
- I am going to start …
- I am going to change the way I …

A WORKED EXAMPLE

- I was late handing in my homework and got detention.
- The causes are:
  - I left it to the last minute.
  - I have a part-time job.
  - I spend a lot of time gaming on the computer at home.
- I can have a direct influence on these causes.

- This is my responsibility.
- I could:
  - give up my job
  - spend less time on the computer
  - do homework as I get it
  - prioritise what is important versus what I want!
- Prioritising the important activities is most appropriate.

- I am going to continue my job.
- I am going to stop spending so much time on the computer.
- I am going to start managing my time more effectively.
- I am going to change the way I think and become more self-disciplined … 'short-term pain for long-term gain'.

Activity 1 Taking personal responsibility

Individually:
a) Think of a couple of situations where you have had to or may in the future have to take personal responsibility for your actions. Use the framework above to structure your thinking and make notes of what you did/will do at each stage.

In pairs:
b) Discuss your experience/plan with a partner, using the following questions as prompts.

- What affects how responsible you are?
- How do you decide what you should or should not be responsible for?
- What does it feel like to take personal responsibility for something or someone?
- Is it possible to take too much responsibility?
- What might be the dangers of taking too much responsibility?

It is important to be able to judge what is reasonable in terms of personal responsibility and what is not reasonable. This is not straightforward and will depend on many things such as age, experience and the situation. Taking personal responsibility means taking control of things that you *can* control. However, you need to be realistic and recognise that there will be certain things that you *cannot* control at different stages in your life or indeed ever!

Activity 2 Deciding the right level of personal responsibility

Consider the scenarios below. Copy the personal responsibility continuum and place each scenario on it depending on whether you think this is being over-responsible, under-responsible or appropriately responsible.

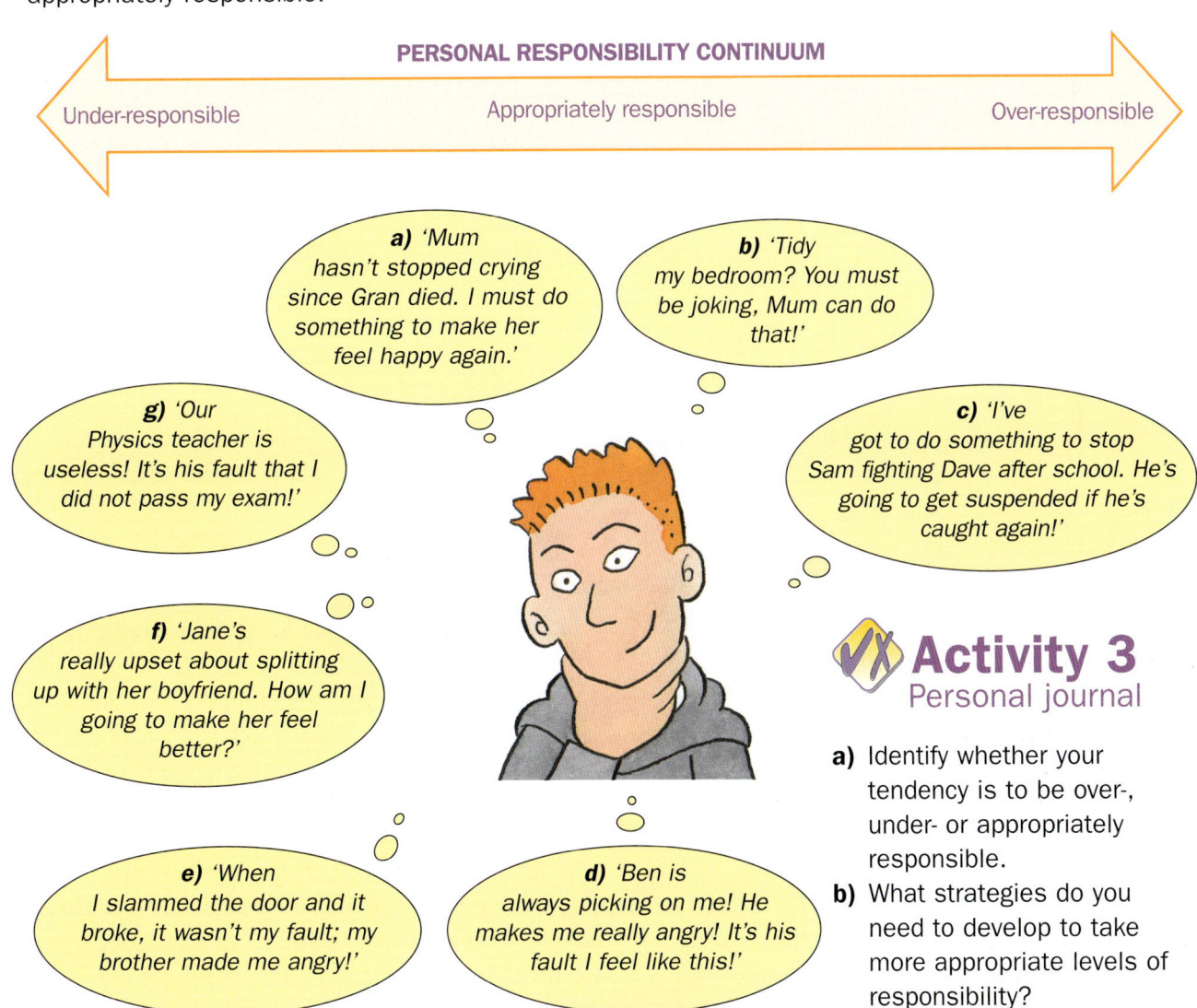

PERSONAL RESPONSIBILITY CONTINUUM

Under-responsible ← Appropriately responsible → Over-responsible

a) 'Mum hasn't stopped crying since Gran died. I must do something to make her feel happy again.'

b) 'Tidy my bedroom? You must be joking, Mum can do that!'

c) 'I've got to do something to stop Sam fighting Dave after school. He's going to get suspended if he's caught again!'

g) 'Our Physics teacher is useless! It's his fault that I did not pass my exam!'

f) 'Jane's really upset about splitting up with her boyfriend. How am I going to make her feel better?'

e) 'When I slammed the door and it broke, it wasn't my fault; my brother made me angry!'

d) 'Ben is always picking on me! He makes me really angry! It's his fault I feel like this!'

Activity 3 Personal journal

a) Identify whether your tendency is to be over-, under- or appropriately responsible.

b) What strategies do you need to develop to take more appropriate levels of responsibility?

Personal Development

7

4 HOW DO I MANAGE IMPULSES?

Learning intentions

I am learning:
- what body impulses are
- how to manage my body impulses by developing self-control.

Many times a day your body talks to you through impulses as you respond to the various stimuli both within you and all around you. A key life skill is to learn when and when not to listen to these impulses, so that you control them rather than have them controlling you. We need self-control to ensure we have legitimate needs met, but avoid being blown about by every whim, or worse, getting into trouble or developing addictions.

Activity 1 Exploring my level of self-control

a) Think through the last 24 hours. List all the impulses you have experienced in your body. The diagram below will help give you some ideas.

b) Divide the list into the things you feel:
- are appropriate to respond to
- you need to manage more carefully or postpone, and
- you should not respond to.

c) Think through one or two specific examples, particularly of impulses that you regularly give in to. Describe the process of what stimulates you, what happens inside and outside your body, and how you respond in your thinking and behaviour.

d) How self-controlled would you say you are?

I need a drink. / I'm hungry. / I need comfort. / I need a hug. / I need somebody to love. / I need to go to the toilet. / I need to avoid pain and discomfort. / I need chocolate. / I need more than this! / I need to tell lies. / I am so angry. / I need to scream! / I need to be liked.

For many years people have thought that all you need to control body impulses is strong willpower or the threat of sanctions from parents, community, school or society. The trouble is, this has never worked! This is because even if we don't give in to an impulse, the level at which our bodies respond stays the same throughout most of our lives. We cannot control how our bodies respond to stimuli, but we can control the influence the impulse has on us. This is a subtle but important difference!

Body impulse = **Things that stimulate us** + **Our thinking** + **The context of a given moment**

We cannot change whether or not we have body impulses, but to control them we can manage the three influences (the thing that stimulates us, the way we think about the stimulus and the environment we are in when we feel the impulse). There are two different strategies we can apply:

1) **Reduce** the stimulation so that it loses its power.
   - Substitute a different behaviour as a diversion; for instance, whenever you want to snack, do physical exercise instead.
   - Change the physical environment that the impulse relies on; for instance, if you want to give up smoking, don't carry or buy cigarettes any more.

2) **Energise** a different, positive competing impulse to replace the negative one. The new impulse is more attractive and its energy dominates the negative impulse. This is usually a long-term, slow but effective process; for instance, learning to play the guitar instead of watching useless TV. This takes thinking, planning, purchasing, organising, practising and developing, so over time it dominates the negative impulse.

Activity 2
Developing strategies for self-control

In pairs:
a) Pick two activities that create body impulses that you find difficult to control from the examples below or think of another example.
b) Formulate strategies to reduce or energise the influence they have on you so that you can develop better self-control.
c) Encourage your partner by suggesting as many strategies to help as possible.

Nail biting

Thumb sucking

Smoking

Over- or under-eating

Playing computer games

Watching TV

Eating chocolate

Drinking alcohol

Personal Development

9

5 HOW CAN I BECOME BETTER AT PLANNING?

Learning intentions

I am learning:
- ✓ how to create an action plan
- ✓ how being organised can help me learn better.

Planning is an essential process for successfully achieving goals. It can be very simple (for example, deciding what clothes to wear to go on a school trip) or more complex (for example, organising an end-of-term party for the local youth club). Whatever type of planning you may be involved in, there is a process that can be followed that will help you plan more successfully and learn something about yourself and your own organisational skills in the process. This process, outlined in the diagram below, is called the 'action planning cycle'.

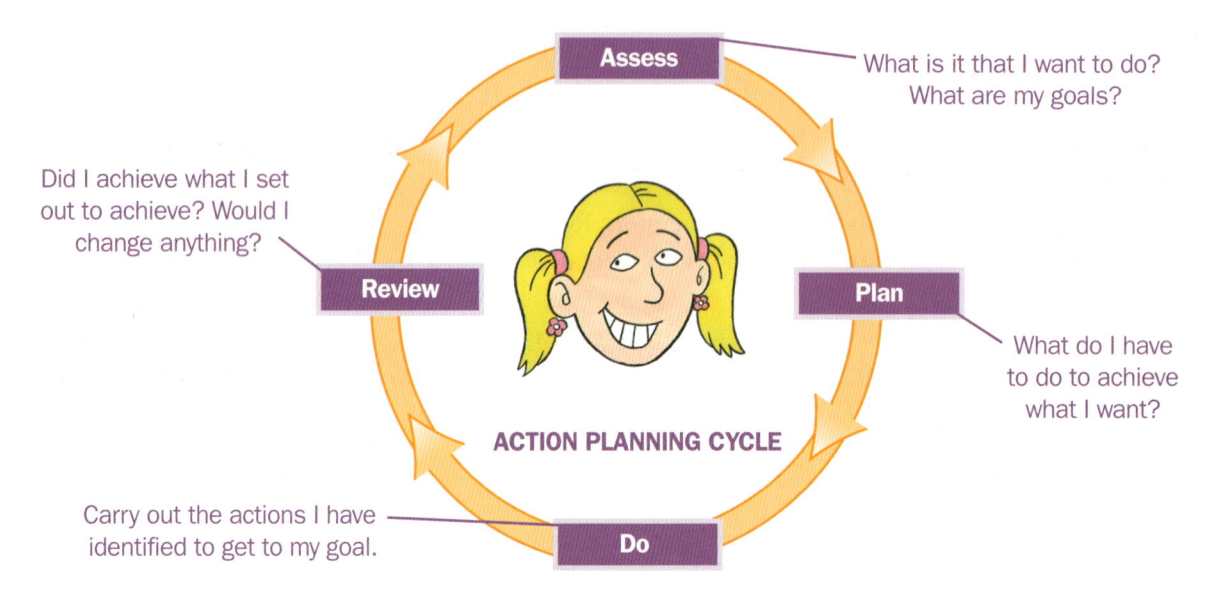

ACTION PLANNING CYCLE

- **Assess** — What is it that I want to do? What are my goals?
- **Plan** — What do I have to do to achieve what I want?
- **Do** — Carry out the actions I have identified to get to my goal.
- **Review** — Did I achieve what I set out to achieve? Would I change anything?

Many people think an action plan is complete after they have carried out all the activities identified in the plan (the 'do' stage). However, it is important to reflect on the success of the plan (the 'review' stage) to help you learn and become a better planner next time.

Activity 1 Making an action plan

There are lots of different templates to choose from for action planning. Which template is best may well depend on the task you are doing. The one shown on page 11 is a good starting point and can be adapted to suit your needs if appropriate.

a) Use the action planning template to plan an event.

- Choose an event to plan, for example: choosing subject options, carrying out a project, creating a revision programme for exams, a day trip or a party.
- Copy the action planning template into your book or design a similar one on a computer.

Personal Development

10

- Use the prompt questions in the template to guide your thinking and complete an action plan for your event. Use the exemplification in the template as a guide when completing your own action plan.

b) Follow your action plan to carry out the event.
c) After the event, evaluate how successful your plan was.

Action planning template

Assess
What is my starting point or baseline? What is the current situation? What do I want to achieve and why?
For example: 1. My bedroom is a mess. 2. Mum says I have to tidy it or my pocket money will stop. 3. I have to have it tidied by teatime.
Plan
What is the best way to get to where I want to be? Use SMART targets (**S**pecific, **M**easurable, **A**chievable, **R**ealistic, **T**ime-bound).
For example: 1. Sort out the rubbish from what I want to keep. 2. Organise my wardrobe to make space for the clothes on the floor. 3. Find somewhere to keep my CDs and magazines. 4. Clean my room so that it will pass Mum's inspection!
Implement
How will I put my plan into action? When might there be a need for flexibility in my plan?
For example: 1. Get black plastic bags and throw out any rubbish. 2. Sort through my clothes and put anything that I don't wear into a bag for the charity shop. 3. Vacuum the floor, tidy and dust the shelves. 4. Put all my CDs and magazines into the space I have created on my shelf. 5. Call Mum up to inspect my room before tea.
Evaluate
Did I do the right things? Did I do things right? What would I do differently next time?
For example: Room passed Mum's inspection, but I should have cleared out my cupboards as well and I forgot to look under the bed and missed some CDs that had been kicked under there. Next time I would clear everything off the floor onto my bed, sort it out, throw out the rubbish and then vacuum the floor, including under the bed. I would also get a damp cloth and wipe down my shelves as the duster would not remove the sticky marks left by a Coke can.

Activity 2
Personal journal

a) How did using the template affect the planning of your event?
b) Consider how you could modify the template so that it better suits your needs.
c) What were the advantages to using a clearly defined process when planning for an event?

Personal Development

6 HOW DO I THINK CRITICALLY?

Learning intentions

I am learning:
- what it means to be a critical thinker
- how to apply critical thinking to problems in my life.

A person who thinks critically uses their ability to reason, reflect and act responsibly when deciding what to believe or do. They ask appropriate questions, gather and sort relevant information, reason logically and come to reliable and trustworthy conclusions about their actions. Many of these skills you will have used before. In this topic you are going to try and pull them together and practise becoming a better critical thinker.

Critical thinking involves thinking logically based on facts that you know and evidence from reliable sources to ensure decisions are not made on the basis of biased opinions. It includes the ability to make comparisons between information, to sequence or classify information and identify patterns such as cause and effect. There are many ways of learning to think critically. Below is one framework which helps to structure thinking in a way that applies the principles of critical thinking to problem solving. It is based on a classification system (or taxonomy) developed by an educational psychologist called Benjamin Bloom.

- Reasoning skills
- Enquiry skills
- Evaluation skills
- Information-processing skills
- Creative thinking skills

Critical thinker

1) **Knowledge**
   - What do I know?
   - What factual information do I have?

2) **Comprehension**
   - What do I understand from these facts?
   - What consequences or meanings are linked to these facts?

3) **Application**
   - How can I apply this information to a new situation?
   - Is there any problem I can solve?
   - How could I do this?

4) **Analysis**
   - What happened when I applied my ideas?
   - Why did this happen?
   - Can I explain any patterns or trends in what happened when I applied my ideas?

5) **Synthesis (pulling it all together)**
   - Can I come up with possible 'what if' scenarios that apply to the situation being considered?
   - Can I come up with some new ideas to apply to the situation being considered?

6) **Evaluation**
   - Can I describe what is good or successful, and what is not so good or successful, about the suggested solutions?
   - Can I make suggestions to improve the situation?
   - Can I offer alternative approaches or other questions to consider?

Six steps to critical thinking

Activity 1 Becoming a critical thinker

1) Should I buy cheaper 'value' products rather than branded products?

2) Who should I vote for in the school council elections?

3) Which mobile network should I use?

4) What's the best way to achieve a healthy body?

a) Choose one of the problems above or think of one of your own.
b) Apply the 'six steps to critical thinking' framework to structure your thinking as you work through the problem.
c) Find the information you need to make informed decisions about possible solutions.
d) Copy and complete the table to help you.

Process	Steps involved
Analyse the problem What is the problem?	1 and 2
Generate possible solutions What could work?	3
Choose one possible solution and try it out How will I do it?	4 and 5
Evaluate how successful it was What worked? What could be improved?	6

Activity 2 Personal journal

a) Identify two occasions where you have used some of these skills to solve problems in your everyday life.
b) How did being more critical help you make better decisions?
c) What makes using a critical thinking process challenging?
d) What do you see as the advantages to using the skills of critical thinking for your future?

Personal Development

13

7 HOW CAN I DEVELOP REFUSAL SKILLS?

Learning intentions

I am learning:
- to understand when to say yes and when to say no to choices in my life
- to develop and use refusal skills when necessary.

We know that not everything in life is good for us. Developing the wisdom to know what to accept or reject is important, but knowledge is not enough. It is equally important to have the skills to accept or refuse life's possibilities. It is important to practise these skills before you get into the middle of a difficult situation!

Activity 1 Exploring possibilities

In groups:
a) Make a list of all the potential new choices and possibilities that are becoming part of life for you now as teenagers.
b) Organise your list into two categories: possibilities you want to say yes to, and others you want to refuse.

Refusal skills are a set of skills designed to help you have fun, keep friends and also stay out of trouble by avoiding participation in high-risk, negative behaviours. They can enable you to resist peer pressure while maintaining self-respect and they develop self-control. Consider this five-step model for developing the skill of refusal.

3) Identify consequences

If you take part in this activity, what are you risking? Think through the entire consequences: legal, social, health, personal, emotional, spiritual, environmental.

2) Name the trouble

Vagueness is not helpful. What is the trouble that you want to avoid? Base your decision on accurate, not faulty, information. Is this right or wrong for you?

4) Suggest alternatives

The important thing is not to get into an argument. You are not trying to prove you are right, but to maintain your boundaries and avoid trouble. You want to suggest a positive alternative and get out of the situation as quickly and smoothly as possible. How you do this will depend on you, the situation and the people you are with. Remember that *how* you say it is as important as *what* you say.

1) Ask questions

Is this activity something you want to do or not? The key here is actually to stop and think. Most often we drift into trouble without realising it!

5) Leave and leave the door open

It is better not to threaten or put down the person or group tempting you. If they persist, it is best to leave. If possible leave the friendship or relationship open. In extreme cases, you may need to question whether the relationship has a future or not.

Based on 'Handy refusal skills' by David Hawkins

Personal Development

14

Activity 2 Practising refusal skills

In groups:
- Use the lists you made in Activity 1.
- Each pick one of the issues you don't want in your life.
- Refer to the five-step refusal model to prompt thinking and improvising.
- Take turns to create scenarios where the other members of the group try to pressure you to do the thing you don't want to do. Practise a variety of strategies for saying no. Use the suggestions below to help you.
- Act out the best scenario in front of the whole class.

Strategies for refusing

- Come up with another idea.
- Use humour.
- Call it what it is.
- Simply ignore what is being said.
- Switch topics.
- Don't accuse.
- Use an excuse.
- Challenge the speaker. (Be careful; however sometimes you can help the whole group to make a healthier choice.)
- Turn the tables. Take the pressure off you and put it on the person suggesting the activity.
- Be polite.
- Walk away. Sometimes it is best to say nothing, and simply get out.
- Anything else?

Activity 3
Personal journal

a) Identify three negative areas in your life that are difficult for you to resist.
b) What strategies and refusal skills do you need to practise to reduce your risk of giving in and with whom?

Personal Development

8 HOW DO I MOTIVATE MYSELF?

Learning intentions

I am learning:
- ✓ what internal and external motivation means
- ✓ practical ways to motivate myself and others.

Activity 1 Who is responsible for my GCSE results?

In groups:
- Read through the statements below.
- Decide if you agree or disagree with each one.
- Debate the issue together and see if you can persuade the rest of your group to agree with you by giving a convincing rationale and argument.

a) The GCSE grades a person gets is under their own control.

b) Government, parents and teachers should force children to study for two hours per night in Years 11 and 12 – then GCSE results would improve.

c) The GCSE grades I get are mostly dependent on how good my teacher is.

d) My GCSE results depend on how smart I start out, not on whether I work hard.

What is motivation?

The word 'motivation' comes from the Latin verb 'movere' = to move. When motivated, we are moved by a reason or reasons to engage in, or avoid, a particular behaviour. There are many different reasons behind our behaviours, such as enjoyment, fear, coercion, addiction, pleasure, obligation, duty, suffering, justice, revenge and so on. We all need a basis to motivate ourselves to persevere and keep going when things are tough. So where does motivation come from?

There are two broad types of motivation: internal and external.

Internal motivation is when we motivate ourselves from within, creating our own internal reasons for our actions or inaction.

External motivation is when the reasons for our behaviour are created or imposed on us by others (family, friends, teachers, enemies, government, circumstances, advertisers, and so on).

Becoming an adult means taking more responsibility for self-motivation (= independence) rather than relying on others to motivate you (= dependence). It also means knowing when to ask for help and utilise others to help motivate you (= interdependence).

Personal Development

16

The panels contain factors that can positively motivate yourself or others. Use the suggestions to help develop strategies that work for you.

Motivating yourself
- Pleasure
- All types of reward
- Creating manageable steps
- Setting short-, medium- and long-term goals
- Exploring consequences
- Recognition
- Discipline
- Kindness
- Money
- Personal responsibility
- Challenging yourself
- Self-respect
- Being creative
- Self-fulfilment
- Stimulation
- Moral obligation
- Proving something
- Giving something back
- Values

Motivating others
- Various rewards (e.g. money)
- Helping self/others
- Spelling out consequences
- Giving detailed instructions to follow
- Kindness
- Setting deadlines for others to keep
- Creating team spirit (interdependence)
- Trust/faith
- Creating challenges for people to rise to
- Vision
- Appraisal and constructive criticism
- Demands or threats
- Sanctions
- Fun
- Communication
- Stimulating excitement
- Laws and rules
- Loyalty

Activity 2 Olympic training

Choose an Olympic sportsperson whom you admire. Research what sort of things they need to do in their life in order to participate in their sport at the Olympics. See if you can find out what motivates them to do all this training and preparation – is it internal or external motivation, or both?

Activity 3 Picking GCSEs

In pairs:
a) Identify GCSE subjects that motivate you.
- Why do they motivate you?
- What subjects demotivate you? Why?

b) Make a list of the GCSE results you hope for. (Be specific – don't be vague!)
c) What motivation (internal and external) will you need to get the results you hope for?
d) Create a plan that maps out the motivating factors you need using ideas from the two panels above.
- What do you need to do to motivate yourself?
- Who do you need to ask to help motivate you and why?

Activity 4 Personal journal

a) Can you motivate yourself? What evidence in the last month is there to prove this?
b) Do you rely on others motivating you too much or too little?
c) What percentages of the following activities are internally or externally motivated for you?
- Getting up in the morning
- Doing housework (cooking, cleaning, ironing, washing, and so on)
- Studying
- Eating healthily
- Exercise

d) Would your family answer in the same way? Find out by asking them.
e) In which areas of your life would you like to be more independent? How could you organise and motivate yourself more appropriately?
f) In which areas of your life do you need to ask for help and be more interdependent?

Personal Development

9 HOW DO I MANAGE PERSONAL CHANGE?

Learning intentions
I am learning:
- that change is inevitable and important
- about my capacity for change
- to develop the skill of managing change in my life.

Activity 1
My capacity to change

a) Have you ever made a New Year's resolution? If so, did you keep it? If not, why not?

b) Can you think of any habit or personal transformation you have made? How did you change, or if not, why did you find change difficult?

Based on the 'Stages of change model' by James Prochaska/Carlo DiClemente (1982)

Experts are suggesting that there will be as much change in the next three decades as there was in the last three centuries! We are now in a period of continuous change on an accelerating time cycle. If we are not just going to survive but actually enjoy life and make the most of it, we need to be people who can manage change. This is not just change in society or globally, but most importantly, in ourselves. So, can you adapt and change?

You would think personal change would be simple and straightforward – it definitely isn't! Stopping biting your nails, giving up smoking, or keeping up an exercise regime are all difficult. Change doesn't happen easily or without careful and thoughtful effort.

People move through different stages on their way to successful change. We will all progress in our own time at a pace we are comfortable with, because stable, long-term change cannot be imposed by someone else. In each of the stages, a person has to grapple with a different set of issues and tasks, so different tools and strategies are needed to achieve lasting change successfully.

The stages of change are:

1) **Problem – not me!**
   In the beginning we often do not see that there is a problem attitude or behaviour that needs to be changed. This can be realistic, because there is no problem, or an avoidance of reality, sometimes called 'denial'.

2) **I might just take a look at my life …**
   Next we acknowledge that there is an issue or problem, but we are not yet ready, or sure of wanting to do anything, to make a change.

3) **I'm going to do something**
   We develop a determination to change and prepare by creating a change plan.

4) **Doin' the stuff**
   Now we take action, using willpower and changing attitudes and behaviour.

STAGES OF CHANGE

- Lasting exit
- 5 Keeping the stuff going
- 6 Whoops! Falling backwards
- Enter
- 1 Problem? – Not me!
- 4 Doin' the stuff
- 3 I'm going to do something
- 2 I might just take a look at my life …

Personal Development

18

5) **Keeping the stuff going**
   We need to maintain the attitude and behaviour change over a period of time until it becomes our new way of operating. Usually it takes between 21 and 80 days to form a new habit, i.e. lasting change.
6) **Whoops! Falling backwards**
   Because change is difficult, we may return to older attitudes and behaviours, abandoning the new changes.

Notice this is circular. We may have to go through the stages several times before we achieve lasting change.

Activity 2 Defining and exploring personal change

In groups:
a) Go back to Activity 1. Use the stages of change model opposite to help explain why you did or didn't change.
b) Choose three activities that are relevant or challenging for you (from the following examples or your own ideas). Give a rationale of what stage of change you are in.

Eating healthily

Gossiping and putting down others

Revising for exams

Smoking cigarettes

Doing regular exercise

Having a racist attitude

Drinking alcohol

c) Think through each of the change stages. What strategies would you use to help someone who was stuck and unable to make progress with change? For instance, at stage 1, how would you help someone who is in denial?

Activity 3 Personal journal

a) How would you describe your capacity to change?
b) Is there any issue, attitude or behaviour that you want or need to change? What would your friends or family say? (Why not ask them?)
c) What do you need to do to move yourself through each stage to lasting change?

10 WHAT RISK DOES ALCOHOL PRESENT FOR TEENAGERS?

Learning intentions

I am learning:
- about potential risks created by alcohol
- how to develop prevention and safety strategies around alcohol.

In this topic you will look at research around alcohol and the risks it presents for teenagers. The point of doing the research will be to put together a brochure that is relevant, real and engaging for the pupils in your school.

To provide a structure for the research and brochure, use the 'I AM' risk management process in the diagram below. 'I AM' can help you remember the three key steps in the process of risk management:

- **Identify** the risk around alcohol.
- **Assess** the level of risk of it actually happening in reality.
- **Manage** the risk by preventing or reducing the risk to a level where the event is extremely unlikely to happen.

Drink awareness advertisement

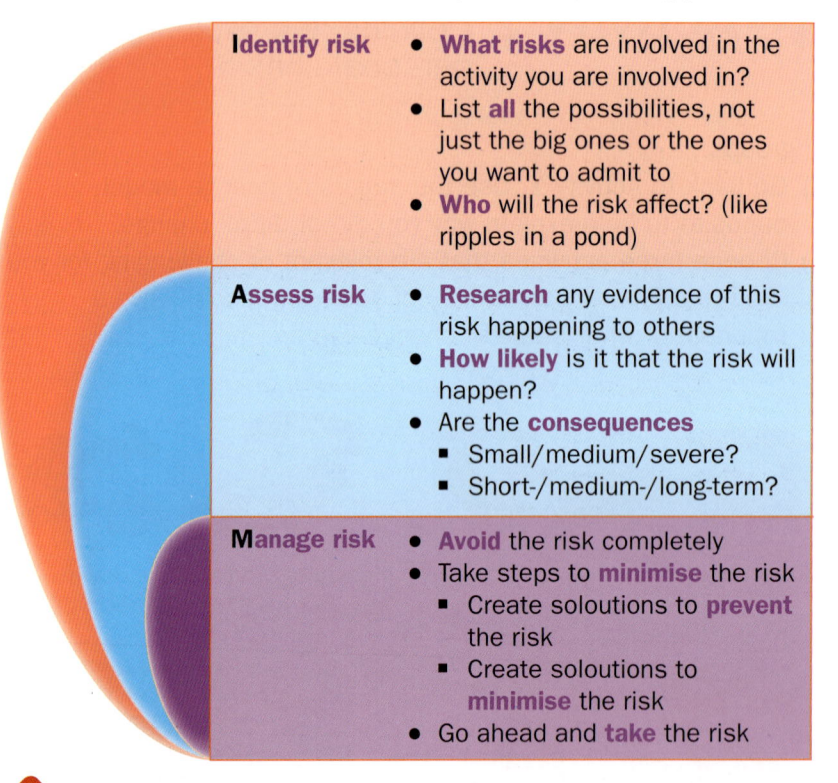

Identify risk	• **What risks** are involved in the activity you are involved in? • List **all** the possibilities, not just the big ones or the ones you want to admit to • **Who** will the risk affect? (like ripples in a pond)

Assess risk	• **Research** any evidence of this risk happening to others
	• **How likely** is it that the risk will happen?
	• Are the **consequences**
	  ▪ Small/medium/severe?
	  ▪ Short-/medium-/long-term?

Manage risk	• **Avoid** the risk completely
	• Take steps to **minimise** the risk
	  ▪ Create soloutions to **prevent** the risk
	  ▪ Create soloutions to **minimise** the risk
	• Go ahead and **take** the risk

Activity 1 Identifying the risks around alcohol for teenagers

In groups:
a) The first task is to write down all the possible risks around alcohol. Don't evaluate them at this stage; just make a list of any of the possibilities.
b) Use a variety of means to get the information, for instance:
   ▪ what your group already knows
   ▪ the internet
   ▪ local drugs agencies and charities
   ▪ government campaigns through health promotion.

Police arresting binge-drinking teenagers outside a nightclub

c) Think through all the effects of alcohol on the whole person, i.e.

- physically
- socially and relationally
- legally
- sexually
- emotionally
- spiritually
- cognitively, in other words, its effects on thinking, school work or memory
- financially.

Homeless person drinking alcohol on the street

Activity 2 Assessing the risks around alcohol for teenagers

a) From your list in Activity 1, pick out what you think are the top five risks around alcohol for teenagers.

b) Find out the likelihood in percentage terms of some of the most common risks being realised by obtaining relevant statistics. For example, if a teenager drinks a certain amount of alcohol the chances of 'x' happening are 20 per cent or one in five over a year. What is the likelihood of:

- getting in trouble with the police?
- getting into a fight?
- being in a car accident?
- becoming pregnant?
- having health problems?

c) Assess whether each risk is short-, medium- or long-term. What difference does that make?

Activity 3 Managing the risks presented by alcohol

Take your five top risks for teenagers and alcohol, and begin to formulate strategies to manage the risks. Remember, management may include:

- preventing the event from ever happening
- reducing the risk by minimising its chances of happening
- taking the risk and hoping!

Activity 4 Producing a brochure

Now it is time to collate all the information you have pulled together in the previous three activities. You are health promotion agents for a change!

a) Work together in your group and design a brochure that is targeted at teenagers in your school and community. The challenge is to make it factual and accurate, yet at the same time real, relevant and interesting.

b) If appropriate, why not print some out and pass them round the teenagers in your school? Alternatively your group could make a presentation to another group or class about your findings.

Personal Development

1.1 WHAT'S THE DIFFERENCE BETWEEN BEING MALE AND FEMALE?

Learning intentions
I am learning:
- how my identity is linked to gender
- how gender stereotyping affects behaviour
- to be aware of unhelpful gender stereotyping.

Gender is defined as the state of being male or female. We know we are either male or female and usually simply take it for granted. Different cultures and societies define the values, roles and behaviours that are deemed appropriate for males and females in different ways. As we grow up with these expectations from our culture and society, our own sense of being male or female (our gender identity) is reinforced by our individual memories and learning experiences. Therefore, we often develop behaviours that are particularly 'masculine' or 'feminine' without realising it.

Activity 1 What does it mean to be male or female?

a) Get into same-sex pairs or small groups.
b) Divide a large sheet of paper into two and write the headings 'What can males do/not do?' and 'What can females do/not do?' at the top of each column.
c) Brainstorm all your ideas onto the page. Don't worry about being right or wrong; write down everything.
d) Now compare your sheet with that of another group, preferably one of the opposite sex.
e) Discuss the following questions in your group.

- Are there any big differences between the two sheets of information?
- What do you think causes these differences in interpretation?
- Could different interpretations of gender identity cause problems now or in the future? What might these be?
- Are there advantages to being male? If so, what are they?
- Are there advantages to being female? If so, what are they?
- Are the answers to these questions the same for boys and girls? Can you give an explanation for this?

Gender stereotypes of young children

The first thing most people ask of a newborn baby is 'Is it a boy or a girl?' Depending on the answer the baby is likely to be treated differently from that moment on. When we make judgements and decisions based on gender and an expectation of how gender roles should be expressed, we are creating stereotypes. 'Gender stereotyping' is the way people think 'others' should behave just because they are male or female.

Activity 2 Congratulations! It's a baby … !

a) Imagine you are going to visit a family who has just had a baby.
b) Think about the differences you might expect to see and hear for a baby girl or a baby boy. Use the illustrations on the right as prompts – which are for boys and which are for girls?
c) For each category in the list below say what you think might differ for baby boys and baby girls. Add any additional categories that you think of.

- Type of presents
- Type of clothes
- Colour of clothes
- Type of toys
- What games would be played?
- What types of words would you use to talk to the baby?
- What words would you use to describe the baby?

d) Explain what you have found out about yourself by doing this activity.

- What influenced your responses to the categories for boys and girls?
- Where do you think these influences have come from?

e) Gender stereotyping can sometimes lead to discriminatory behaviour. Look at the pictures below.

- What is your instant reaction to each of them?
- Is this a positive or negative reaction?
- How might this affect your behaviour towards that person?

Activity 3
Personal journal

a) In your experience, are boys and girls treated differently? When and how?
b) Do you agree with the differences in treatment? Why?
c) Is there something you would like to do (for example, a sport or a job) that you feel you can't because you are male or female? What can you do about this?

Personal Development

23

12 HOW DO I DEAL WITH LONELINESS?

Learning intentions

I am learning:
- what factors contribute to loneliness
- to develop strategies to help myself and others manage loneliness.

There are currently nearly seven billion people on the planet. Despite a world so full of people, we have many people who are isolated, lonely and disconnected. In this topic you will explore what loneliness is, what causes it and how we can manage it in ourselves and in those around us.

Activity 1 Defining and exploring loneliness

In groups:
a) What is the difference between being alone and being lonely?
b) Make a list of all the causes of loneliness that you can think of.
c) Do you think it is important to be alone and apart from other people at times?
d) Do you ever feel lonely? Why?
e) When you feel lonely, what do you do that helps?

Activity 2 Dear Aunt Annie …

In pairs:
Imagine you are employed by a teenage magazine to write the responses for the 'Agony Aunt Annie' column. Read the letter and in a short paragraph make a helpful, succinct response.

AGONY AUNT ANNIE

Dear Aunt Annie,

I am a rather plump, but likeable, 14-year-old girl. The trouble is no-one talks to me! What is wrong with everybody else? I wait in school for them to be my friends, but nobody comes. I feel a deep inner ache that I don't know what to do with, and the only thing that takes it away is eating chocolate. Can you help me?

Lonely from Larne

Why do we feel lonely?

Being alone is about location and the closeness or distance of other people from us. Loneliness is a complex mixture of all the parts that make us up, creating a deep, and often painful, feeling of isolation. It might include:

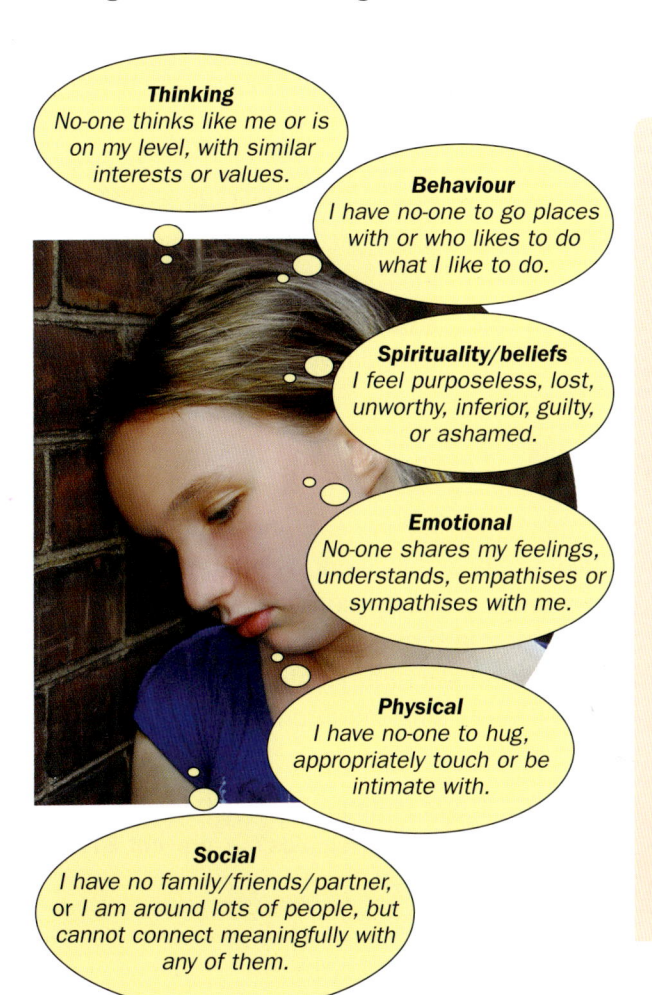

Thinking
No-one thinks like me or is on my level, with similar interests or values.

Behaviour
I have no-one to go places with or who likes to do what I like to do.

Spirituality/beliefs
I feel purposeless, lost, unworthy, inferior, guilty, or ashamed.

Emotional
No-one shares my feelings, understands, empathises or sympathises with me.

Physical
I have no-one to hug, appropriately touch or be intimate with.

Social
I have no family/friends/partner, or I am around lots of people, but cannot connect meaningfully with any of them.

Suggestions for coping with loneliness

1) Build your inner life. Take time to be in solitude, but not lonely.
2) Stay tuned to your body and your feelings so that you can recognise and admit if and when you feel lonely. Don't deny your feelings – face them and manage them. Discuss your loneliness with others.
3) Reduce your social isolation. Don't wait for others; go, meet and interact with them.
4) Go to various groups. Volunteer. Check out clubs in your school or community.
5) Monitor your negative self-talk. Think positively and learn to like yourself.
6) Determine when and in what context you feel most alone and rearrange things to manage this better.
7) Develop solo activities that can be enjoyed.
8) Do things you haven't done before that you didn't think you could do yourself. Then celebrate your success!

Activity 3 Challenging loneliness together

Get back into your groups. Using your new understanding and the suggestions above, suggest two strategies to begin to challenge loneliness in your class/school.

Activity 4 Secret angels

Everyone in your class should put their name in a hat. Each pick out one name, but don't tell anyone who you get. Over the next week, become that person's secret angel. Make them feel included, encouraged, and fulfil their four needs for attention, acceptance, appreciation and affection. After one week, see who can guess who their angel was. Share the impact of your actions.

Personal Development

13 | WHAT ARE THE PROS AND CONS OF USING CONTRACEPTION?

Learning intentions

I am learning:
- ✓ about the different types of contraception
- ✓ why people use contraception
- ✓ about my personal views on using contraceptives.

Birth control or contraception has had a dual purpose in recent times, specifically where condoms are concerned. As well as preventing unwanted pregnancies, condoms can also prevent the spread of sexually transmitted infections, including HIV. However, not all contraceptives do this. There are many forms of contraceptive available. Some are designed for women, others for men, and they work in a variety of ways.

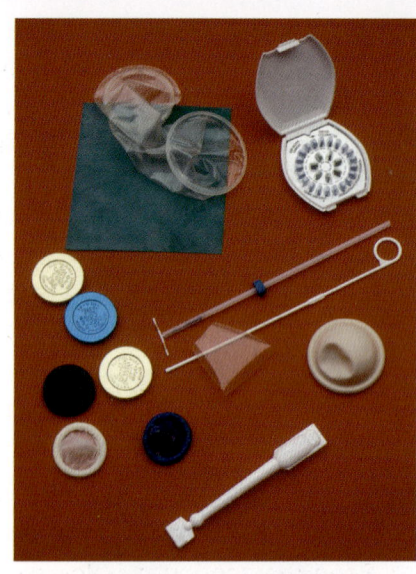

Different types of contraceptives

Activity 1 Types of contraceptives

a) Research as much information as you can about different types of contraceptive and how they work. Leaflets can be obtained from GP surgeries or family planning clinics. Information can be downloaded from websites such as Patient UK (www.patient.co.uk) or KidsHealth (kidshealth.org).

b) Copy and complete the table using the information you collect.

Contraceptive method	How does it work?	How reliable is it?	Is it suitable for males or females?	Does it prevent STIs?
Condoms				
Female condoms				
The pill				
The coil				
The cap or diaphragm				
The withdrawal method				
The rhythm method				
Injections				
The morning-after pill				
Hormonal implants				

Many people have strong feelings about using contraceptives. This may be due to religious beliefs or moral objections to the way that some contraceptives work. Whether to use a contraceptive method or not is a very personal decision and needs careful consideration.

It is important that any person using a contraceptive does so for the right reasons. Once the decision has been made to use a contraceptive, it is important to choose the method that best suits the needs of the particular person or couple.

Activity 3 Choosing contraceptives

a) Imagine you are an agony aunt/uncle of a magazine problem page.
b) Read the scenarios below which contain queries about contraception.
c) For each scenario, use the information you have collected to recommend which contraceptive (if any) the person should use and give a reason for your choice.

Activity 2 Whether to use contraceptives

In pairs:
a) Make a list of positive reasons for deciding to use a contraceptive.
b) Now repeat this process, this time listing negative reasons for using contraceptives.
c) Join with another pair and share your ideas. Discuss any differences of opinion and be prepared to accept that you may not be able to agree.

Dear Agony Aunt …

I am married with four children and have decided that my family is complete. My life is very hectic and I find it difficult to remember to take tablets. I need a method of contraception that is reliable and easy to use. What alternatives are there for my husband and me to consider?

Dear Agony Aunt …

I am in a committed relationship, but neither of us wishes to start a family. I cannot take the pill as it doesn't agree with me. We use condoms at present, but I'm worried as my friend recently discovered she is pregnant and she and her partner always used them. Can you help?

Dear Agony Aunt …

I have been going out with this great girl for six months and we have both decided we are ready to have sex. She told me she is on the pill so I don't have to worry about contraception. I have heard that the pill can sometimes fail if the girl is sick or on other medication. I'm also concerned that she has had sex with other partners and therefore could have an STI. What do you think I should do?

Dear Agony Aunt …

I love my boyfriend very much and we have been having sex for a few months. We have always used condoms, but he wants me to go on the pill because he says it would be easier. How safe is the pill? Are there any downsides? What should I do?

Activity 4 Personal journal

a) Note down three new pieces of information you have learned in this topic.
b) Are there any forms of contraception that you do not agree with? Why?
c) What do you think are the most important things to consider before deciding to use a contraceptive?

Personal Development

14 HOW DO I AVOID SEXUALLY TRANSMITTED INFECTIONS?

Learning intentions

I am learning:
- ✓ about common sexually transmitted infections (STIs)
- ✓ how STIs are acquired
- ✓ strategies to avoid being infected with an STI.

Sexually transmitted infections are not a new medical problem. They have probably been around for as long as people have been having sex and are a problem in any society that indulges in sexual activity.

According to the latest available World Health Organization (WHO) estimates from 1999, 340 million new cases of curable STIs (syphilis, gonorrhoea, chlamydia and trichomoniasis) occur annually throughout the world in adults aged 15 to 49.

These days there is a lot of information available about STIs and safer sex. Leaflets can be obtained from GP surgeries or family planning clinics and information can be downloaded from websites such as the Health Promotion Agency (www.healthpromotionagency.org.uk).

Activity 1 What are STIs?

a) Carry out some independent research to find out as much as you can about STIs. Remember to use your critical thinking skills when assessing the quality of the information you obtain. These websites may be helpful.

- www.kidshealth.org/teen/sexual_health/
- www.need2know.co.uk/health/sexual_health
- www.publichealthmatters.org/hcsexualhealth.htm
- www.patient.co.uk

Leaflets on sexually transmitted infections

b) Use the information you find to copy and complete the table below.

STI	Symptoms	Treatments
Chlamydia		
Gonorrhoea		
Genital herpes		
Genital warts (HPV)		
HIV and AIDS		
Syphilis		
Trichomoniasis		

Researching

Despite their long history, there are still many myths regarding STIs and how they can be caught. This is because many people are too embarrassed to talk or ask questions about STIs, so they often don't know the facts or how to protect themselves properly.

Activity 2 True or false?

a) Use the information you have gathered to decide whether each of the statements below is a myth or a reality. Provide relevant evidence to back up your choice.
b) Compare your answers with those of a partner and discuss any differences or disagreements. Try to resolve these using the combined evidence you and your partner have collected.
c) What other things have you heard about catching STIs? Do you think they are true or false?

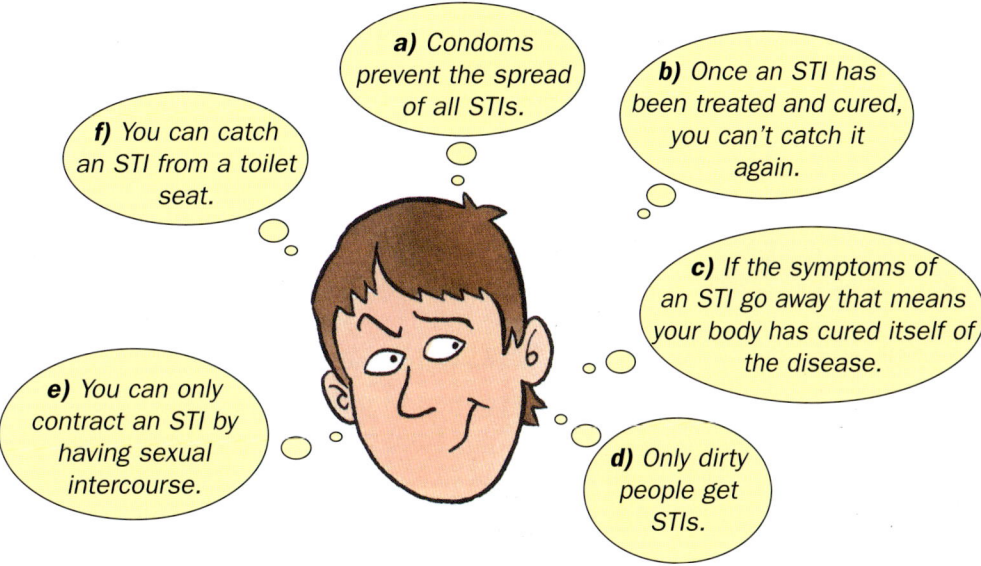

a) Condoms prevent the spread of all STIs.

b) Once an STI has been treated and cured, you can't catch it again.

c) If the symptoms of an STI go away that means your body has cured itself of the disease.

d) Only dirty people get STIs.

e) You can only contract an STI by having sexual intercourse.

f) You can catch an STI from a toilet seat.

It is much better to avoid catching an STI than to have to have one treated. The best way to do this is to abstain from sexual intercourse or to have sexual intercourse only within a long-term relationship where both partners are monogamous and know they are uninfected. When having sexual intercourse with a new partner, the most effective method of reducing the risk of catching or passing on an STI is to use male condoms.

Activity 3 Prevention is better than cure

Using all the information you have obtained in this topic, design and create a 'safer sex' poster that conveys the important messages about safer sex in ways that will appeal to and impact on young people's behaviour.

Activity 4 Personal journal

a) How easy is it to access accurate information about STIs?
b) When do you think many young people should find out about STIs? Before or after they become sexually active? Why?
c) What has been the most important piece of information you have learned from this topic?

Personal Development

15 WHERE CAN I GET HELP IN MY COMMUNITY?

Learning intentions

I am learning:
- how to identify when I need to ask for help
- what external support systems are available
- how to access support when I need it.

Personal Development involves having the internal resources and external support in order to live life effectively. An important aspect of self-management is to know when you need to ask for help, know what you need help with, and be able to identify from whom or where you can get help and how best to go about it.

When things start controlling you, such as anger, stress or drugs, rather than you controlling them, then it may be time to ask for help. We can help ourselves in many ways by developing internal resources such as becoming well organised, learning to think positively and using certain strategies and techniques to help us solve problems or make decisions. However, sometimes we cannot deal with a problem or situation on our own and need external support and help from someone or somewhere else.

Anger

'in control'   'out of control'

Stress

'in control'   'out of control'

Drugs and alcohol

'in control'   'out of control'

Activity 1 What sort of help do young people need?

In pairs:

a) Discuss and note down all the things you think young people might need help with (the cartoons on the left might give you some ideas). Think as widely as possible and don't rule anything out at this stage.

b) Look at the list you have created. Rearrange information, with similar characteristics into categories, for example, health, drugs, careers, and so on, and give each one a title.

c) Now compare your categories with those of another group. Add any categories to your sheet that you had not thought of.

From Activity 1 it should be clear that young people may need help in a wide variety of areas at certain times or in certain situations. Therefore it is important to find out how help can be accessed. The case studies below highlight some of the issues young people face where they need help to deal with them.

> When my parents split up we moved to a new area with my mum. I had to start a new school and found it really hard to make friends. I started to smoke as a way of fitting in and soon I couldn't stop. I knew it was bad for me as my Granddad had died from lung cancer, but no matter how hard I tried, I couldn't stop. Eventually, I asked my form teacher in school if he knew anyone who could help me. He put me in contact with the Ulster Cancer Foundation which runs support groups to help you stop smoking. With support from my family and teacher, I was able to stop, and best of all, I have made some new friends!

I knew there was something wrong when I couldn't bring myself to get out of bed at the weekends. I felt so depressed that life began to have no meaning for me. No one else seemed to understand, until I spoke to our school counsellor who listened and just allowed me to talk about how I was feeling. She encouraged me to tell my parents how I was feeling and get them to take me to the GP. She was great and organised some counselling for me as well as prescribing a short course of antidepressants. I now feel great and have got involved in a youth group which helps me stay positive.

Activity 2 Who can help me?

Type of help needed	People who can help	Places to get help
Study skills	Teachers	School

In groups:
a) Copy the table above onto a large sheet of paper and put your category headings from Activity 1 into the first column.
b) For each of your category headings, brainstorm a list of different places and people that may be able to offer support in this area.
c) Now consider the best way to access this help, for example, via the internet, by phone, by making an appointment, and so on.
d) Complete your table with all the ideas you have generated.
e) Pick an organisation from your list of places to get help and carry out some research to find out more information about it. Use this information to create an advice leaflet or information poster for young people in your area.
f) The points below might help structure your research:

- name of agency/organisation
- where it is based; local or regional centres
- opening times/access
- main areas of support
- other additional types of support available
- special services for young people.

Activity 3 Personal journal

a) Think of one area in your life that you feel you need some help with.
b) Use the answers from Activity 2 to help you identify the people or place best suited to provide you with the help you need.
c) Create an action plan to ensure you get the help you need so that you can move forward in that area of your life.

Personal Development

16 WHAT DO WE MEAN BY DEMOCRACY?

Learning intentions

I am learning:
- ✓ to define the word 'democracy'
- ✓ to evaluate how people can be involved in decision making in a democracy.

One of the main themes in Local and Global Citizenship is 'Democracy and Active Participation'. The next 15 topics will give you an opportunity to explore this theme and in particular to examine how you can play a part in your school and in your community. In this topic you will learn about the idea of democracy.

Activity 1 *Question Time*

a) Imagine you are in the audience of the programme *Question Time*. You ask the panel, 'What does 'democracy' mean to you?'
b) Look at their responses below. Which do you agree with most?
c) How would *you* answer the question?

In groups:

d) Compare your answers to part c) and agree a joint definition.

As a class:

e) Discuss each group's answers and try to agree a class definition.

> *Democracy is a form of government in which the people have a say in what happens either by voting on issues directly or by voting for representatives who take decisions for them.*

> *Democracy is about everyone taking responsibility for their own actions and about being well informed so they can challenge the actions of others – especially those of the Government.*

> *There's more to democracy than just voting. Democracy is about making sure that everyone is treated fairly, is given the same opportunities in life and has their human rights respected.*

What does 'democracy' mean to you?

As you can see from the activity above, an important characteristic of democracy is people having a say or being involved in decision making. This is often called 'citizen participation'. But what is the best way to involve people in making decisions? The next activity should help you answer this question.

Activity 2 Decisions, decisions

1) Inviting a controversial leader to visit Northern Ireland
2) Where to locate a regional sports stadium 
3) How much money to spend on education 
4) Whether to go to war or not 
5) The age at which people can vote 

Imagine a decision needs to be made on the issues above.

In groups:
a) Copy the concept map below which describes four different ways in which a decision could be made about these issues in a democracy.
b) Choose one of the issues above and write it in the middle of your concept map.
c) Discuss the advantages and disadvantages of each of the ways people could be involved (or not!) in making a decision for your chosen issue.
d) Record your discussion by completing the concept map.
e) Share your views with the rest of your class.

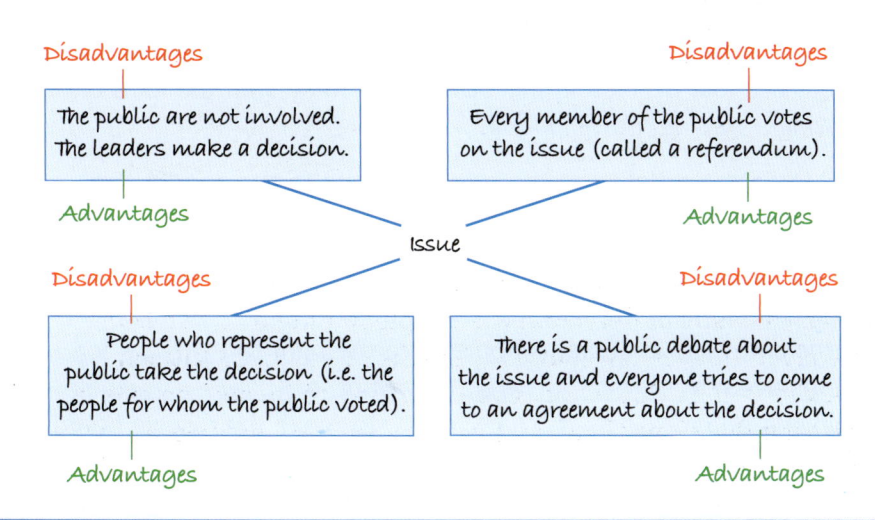

Disadvantages
The public are not involved. The leaders make a decision.
Advantages

Disadvantages
Every member of the public votes on the issue (called a referendum).
Advantages

Disadvantages
People who represent the public take the decision (i.e. the people for whom the public voted).
Advantages

Disadvantages
There is a public debate about the issue and everyone tries to come to an agreement about the decision.
Advantages

Issue

Activity 3
Personal journal

a) What do you think is the most *democratic* way of involving people in the decisions that need to be made?
b) What do you think is the most *practical* way of involving people in the decisions that need to be made?

Local and Global Citizenship

33

17 IS 'PARTICIPATION' A HUMAN RIGHT?

Learning intentions

I am learning:
- ✓ to explain that participation is a human right
- ✓ to collect and manage information to inform others about this human right.

In Book 1 you learned about the Universal Declaration of Human Rights (UDHR) and how this important document contains a list of promises made by governments to all of the citizens of the world. A simplified version of the introduction (or 'preamble') to the UDHR states that:

> *Disrespect for human rights has resulted in barbarous acts which have outraged the conscience of mankind. The greatest hope of all people is to live in a world in which human beings enjoy freedom of speech and belief and freedom from fear and want.*
>
> **UDHR Preamble**

Because governments have signed the UDHR their citizens should expect to have their basic needs met and also expect to have a say in their society.

In this topic you will explore what the UDHR says about the promises governments have made to make sure that people can play a part or participate in their society.

Activity 1 What does the UDHR say about participation?

There are four articles in the UDHR connected with the idea of 'having a say' or 'participating.'

a) Match the articles on the opposite page to the correct cartoons below them.

b) Complete the following sentences.

Participation is more than just the right to v_____. To participate fully in society people have the right to t_____ for themselves, b_____ what they want, e_____ their opinions and j_____ t_____ to make their views heard.

Local and Global Citizenship

*You have the right to **think** and **believe** what you want to and to practise your religion freely.*
Article 18

*You have the right to **express** your opinions freely and nobody should stop you from doing so.*
Article 19

*You have the right to **join together** with others, to take part in meetings and to join associations and to make your views known in a peaceful way.*
Article 20

*You have the right to take part in your country's political affairs. You can be part of the government yourself or can **vote** freely in secret for politicians who have the same ideas as you.*
Article 21

1)   2)   3)   4)

Activity 2 Participation is a human right

a) Find examples to illustrate each of the four UDHR articles above (in local and global contexts) from newspapers, through an internet search or from your knowledge of history or current affairs. Try to find examples of people having (or 'enjoying') this human right as well as examples of people being denied this human right.

b) Prepare a presentation, write a newsletter article, design an informative poster, or organise a school assembly to show that 'Participation is a human right'.

c) Consider how to make your final piece of work more appealing to your 'audience'. You could use:

- images
- song lyrics
- poems
- famous quotations.

d) Organise the information you have gathered and display or present it to your class or school.

Local and Global Citizenship

35

18 DO CHILDREN HAVE A RIGHT TO PARTICIPATE?

Learning intentions

I am learning:
- how governments have promised to allow children to participate in their society
- to evaluate ways in which children's views are listened to.

In Book 1 you learned that governments have made special promises to all the children in the world. These promises, or children's rights, are written down in the United Nations Convention on the Rights of the Child (UNCRC). One very important part of the UNCRC is Article 12 (see below, left).

How can we know if this particular promise is being kept? Dr Laura Lundy works at Queen's University Belfast. She is an expert in children's rights and has constructed a checklist to help us understand what Article 12 really means.

You have the right to say what you think should happen when adults are making decisions that affect you, and to have your opinions taken into account.

Article 12

Article 12
UNCRC

Space
- Is there a safe space for children to express their views? ✓
- Are *all* children included when it comes to hearing their opinions? ✓

Voice
- Are children helped to develop their views? ✓
- Can children express their views directly for themselves? ✓

Audience
- Are children given guaranteed opportunities to express their views? ✓
- Is there someone appointed to listen? ✓

Influence
- Are the views of children taken seriously? ✓
- Are children's views acted upon? ✓
- Do adults take responsibility for responding to children's views even if they have not acted on them? ✓

Dr Laura Lundy, Director, Queen's University Research Forum for the Child
www.qub.ac.uk/child

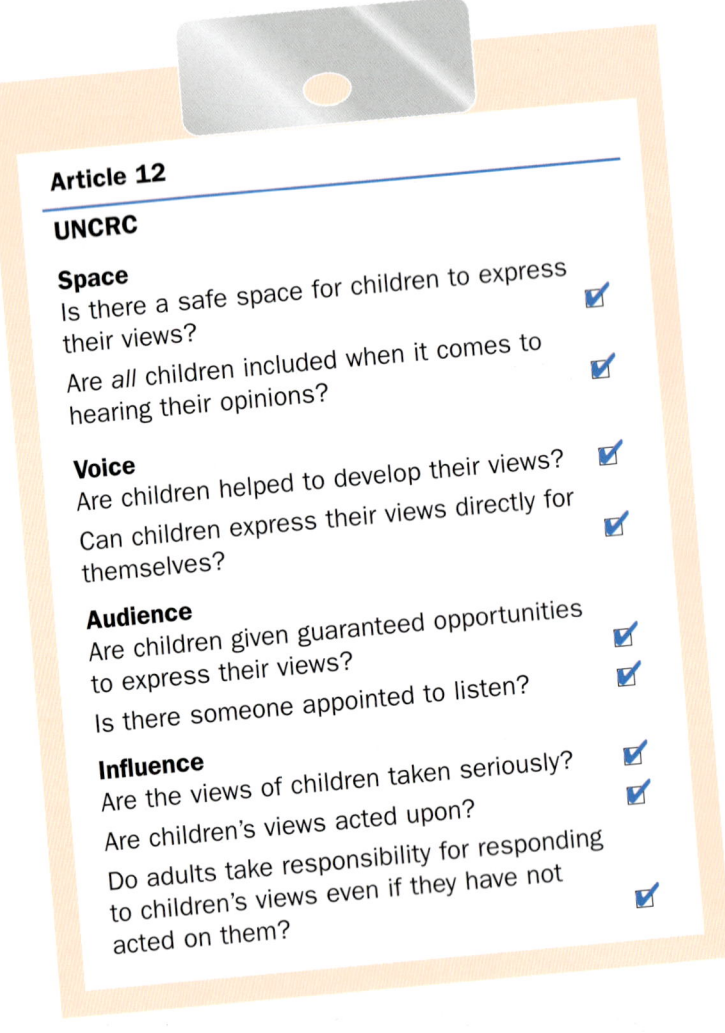

Activity 1 Listening to children?

Imagine your local council has decided to review and upgrade the leisure facilities in the area. It has set aside a sum of money for this, but wants to consult the community about what facilities it would like to have before it makes any decisions. The council is using three approaches to find out the views of local people.

Approach 1: Webpage

Ballyanywhere Local Council
The council wishes to canvas opinion on the regeneration of facilities and amenities in the local area. Please express your views in the box below. These suggestions will be collated and presented to the Council.

Approach 2: Local newspaper

Ballyanywhere Council
The council wishes to find out your views on the upgrading of local leisure facilities in your area. Please tell us what you think by writing to your local councillor. Unfortunately we will not be able to respond to your suggestions.

Approach 3: Poster

Ballyanywhere Council
- Do you care about leisure facilities in your local area?
- How do you think they could be improved?
- We want to hear your views!

Come to Ballyanywhere Community Centre next Thursday at 9 p.m. (Over 18s only)

In groups:
a) Use Laura Lundy's checklist on page 36 to examine each of the approaches taken by the council. Decide how well they ensure that all children's views are being taken into consideration.
b) Could the council find better ways of finding out the views of children on this issue?
c) Write a letter to the council suggesting ways in which it could listen more carefully to the views of children. Use the checklist as a guide to make sure that your suggestions help the council to keep the promise in Article 12 of the UNCRC.

Activity 2
Personal journal

a) Article 12 is only part of the UNCRC that talks about children's right to participate.

- Look at a copy of the UNCRC (you can find an interactive version at www.knowurrights.org/children/know.html). Select all the articles that you think are connected to your right to have a say or take part in your society.

b) Think about your society or community.

- What would you like to have a say about?
- How easy is it for you to express your views?
- What could be done to make sure your views are listened to?

Local and Global Citizenship

19 HOW CAN I PARTICIPATE IN MY SCHOOL?

Learning intentions

I am learning:
- to explain the benefits of participating in school
- about how I can participate in my school.

In the last two topics you discovered that people should *expect* to be able to participate in their society because they have a right to participate. But are there any reasons why people should *want* to participate in society? The next two topics will help you explore the idea of active participation as a social responsibility. In this topic you will explore participation in school.

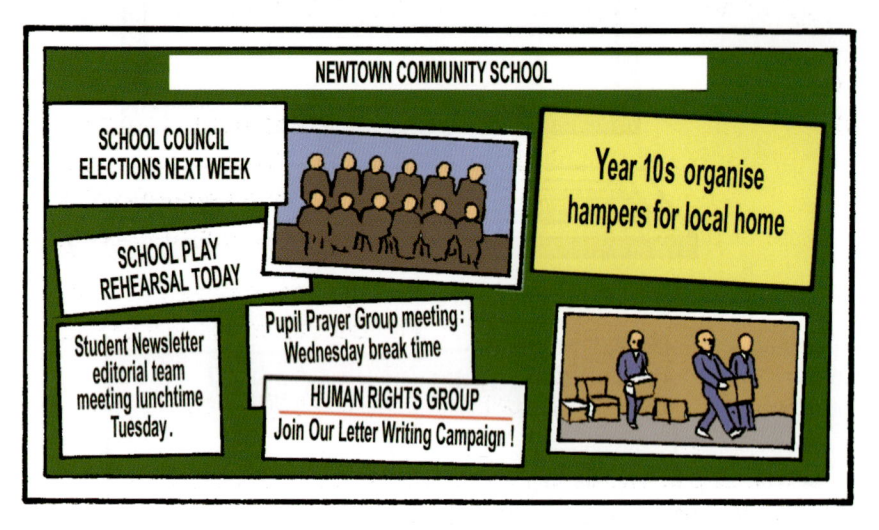

NEWTOWN COMMUNITY SCHOOL

SCHOOL COUNCIL ELECTIONS NEXT WEEK

Year 10s organise hampers for local home

SCHOOL PLAY REHEARSAL TODAY

Student Newsletter editorial team meeting lunchtime Tuesday.

Pupil Prayer Group meeting: Wednesday break time

HUMAN RIGHTS GROUP Join Our Letter Writing Campaign!

Activity 1 Playing a part in school

In groups:

a) Look at the school noticeboard and describe the different ways pupils can play a part in the life of Newtown Community School.

b) Choose at least two of the examples from part a) and explain, for each, how participating in this aspect of school life can:

- help the individual
- help the school
- help the wider community.

c) Share your ideas with the rest of the class and discuss how, *in general*, participating in school benefits the individual, the school and the wider community. Make a large copy of the 'Benefits of participating in school' diagram to record the class discussion.

d) Answer these questions based on what you learned in Topics 17 and 18.

- How does Newtown Community School recognise that pupils have a right to participate?
- Which articles of the UDHR and UNCRC can you see 'in action' on the noticeboard?

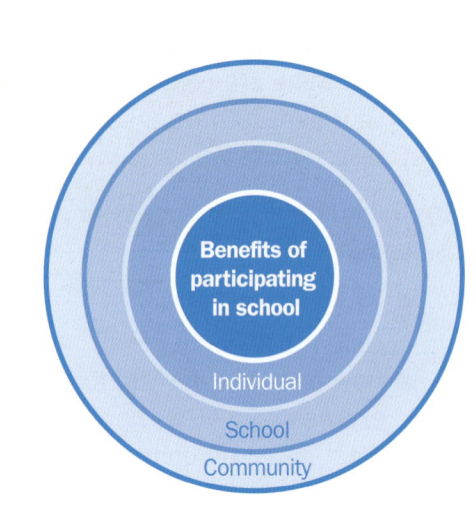

Benefits of participating in school
- Individual
- School
- Community

Local and Global Citizenship

As you will have discovered in Activity 1, above, there are many benefits to participating in school: you can develop skills, contribute to school life and even have an impact on your local community. In the next activity you will evaluate your own school in terms of the opportunities it gives you to play a part.

Activity 2 Auditing participation

Individually:

a) Carry out an audit of your own school to find out how many different opportunities there are for pupils to participate in the life of the school. Write each opportunity on a separate sticky note or piece of paper. Use the following prompts to help you.

- Scan your school newsletter or magazine, prospectus and website and make a note of any opportunities for pupils to participate in school life.
- Walk around your school and examine noticeboards and displays.
- Ask pupils and teachers for examples of opportunities to participate in the life of your school.

In groups:

b) Gather all your 'participation notes' together and try to sort them into categories (such as sport, community service and so on). Decide on the best way to organise the information.

c) Use the following questions to evaluate the opportunities your school provides for participation:

- What types of opportunity does your school provide for pupils to participate?
- Is there a range of opportunities to participate?
- Can everyone find a way to participate if they want to?
- How well does the school encourage participation?
- How could it do better?

d) Present your findings as a report to the school's board of governors.

Activity 3 Personal journal

a) How do you already play an active part in the life of your school?
b) How could you play a more active part in the life of your school?
c) What benefits would there be to participating more in school?

Participating in performing arts

Participating in the school council

Participating in sport

Participating in school community projects

Local and Global Citizenship

39

20 HOW CAN PEOPLE ACTIVELY PARTICIPATE IN THEIR SOCIETY?

Learning intentions

I am learning:
- ✓ about different ways people can participate in their community
- ✓ about the skills associated with active participation.

In Topic 19 you examined different ways to participate in the life of a school. There are also many ways people can participate in their community. By exercising (putting into practice) their right to participate, people can also do something for their community by acting in a socially responsible way.

Activity 1 Active participation in the community

In groups:

a) Look at the street scene and identify and record examples of:

- people participating in the life of their community (local and global).
- other opportunities where people could participate in the life of their community (local and global).

b) Describe examples from the street scene that show people:

- giving their time, money or skills to activities in their community
- trying to influence the decisions of government or other people in authority.

c) Discuss the skills associated with participation and answer the following questions:

- What skills would people need to participate effectively in the activities shown in the street scene?
- What skills could people develop from participating in the activities shown in the street scene?

Activity 2
Personal journal

How would you participate in the street scene community if you lived in it?

- How could you make a difference?
- Would you give time, money or skills to any of the activities in this community?
- What skills do you already have that could help you participate in this community?

Local and Global Citizenship

21. WHO MAKES THE DECISIONS THAT AFFECT ME?

Learning intentions

I am learning:
- who represents me in the local, national and European political institutions
- to research and present information about my representatives.

In Topic 16 you discovered that when you live in a democracy you choose people to represent you and your views. Those people then make decisions on your behalf. However, in Topic 20 you discovered that *everyone* can play their part by contributing to society and by trying to influence those in authority to make good decisions. In the next three topics you will find out who makes these decisions and how to influence them.

In Northern Ireland there are several different places – or political institutions – where our views are put forward by people who represent us. Complete the next activity to find out who represents you.

Activity 1 Who represents me?

- Member of Parliament (MP)
- Councillor
- Member of European Parliament (MEP)
- Member of the Legislative Assembly (MLA)

	Local council, e.g. Belfast City Council	Northern Ireland Assembly	House of Commons (UK government)	European Parliament
Institution				
Location				
Title of representative				
Name(s) of my representatives				

Parliament Buildings, Stormont, Belfast

Belfast City Hall

Palace of Westminster, London

European Parliament, Strasbourg

Local and Global Citizenship

Individually:
a) Copy the table on page 42, leaving space for a fifth row, which you will complete in the next chapter.
b) Complete the second row by recording the correct location of each of the institutions (use the photos on page 42 to help you).
c) Complete the third row by placing the titles of representatives under the correct institution (use the coloured cards on page 42 to help you).
d) Complete the fourth row by finding out the names of your representatives in each of the institutions. You can do this by going to www.wimps.org.uk and typing in your postcode.

In groups:
e) Choose one representative from each of the four institutions. Produce a poster which includes the following for each representative:

- name
- political party
- the institution in which they represent your views
- an example of some of the work they do (for instance, committees they belong to, issues they have voted on, and so on)
- statements they have made.

You can find out more by going to www.theyworkforyou.com or by using a search engine or by visiting their party website.

One of the political institutions mentioned above is the Northern Ireland Assembly. It was set up after the Good Friday/Belfast Peace Agreement. Before this all of the decisions about Northern Ireland were made by the UK government in London. Now your representatives who work in the Assembly can make many decisions about what is best for Northern Ireland. It is sometimes called the 'devolved Assembly' because the power to make decisions on many issues was devolved from (or passed from) the UK government to our local Assembly.

Activity 2
Visit the Northern Ireland Assembly

a) Either ask your teacher to organise a trip to the Northern Ireland Assembly or visit its website (www.niassembly.gov.uk) to find out the answers to these questions:

- Where does the Assembly meet?
- What is the meaning behind the logo (see below)?
- How many representatives are there in the Assembly?
- How many are women?
- Who are the First Minister and Deputy First Minister? What do they do?
- Where does each of the political parties sit in the main chamber?

b) Find out more by trying some of the activities on the Northern Ireland Assembly Education website (education.niassembly.gov.uk).

Assembly Chamber, Parliament Buildings, Stormont, Belfast

Northern Ireland Assembly logo

Local and Global Citizenship

22 | WHAT DECISIONS CAN MY REPRESENTATIVES MAKE?

Learning intentions

I am learning:
- ✓ examples of the issues my representatives discuss in local, national and European political institutions
- ✓ about the types of decisions my representatives make.

In Topic 21 you discovered who represents you in various political institutions. In this topic you will find out about the decisions they can make. There are so many decisions made by politicians that it can sometimes be confusing to work out where the decision was made and by whom. The next activity will help you to understand who makes the different types of decisions.

Activity 1 Sort it out!

LOCAL COUNCIL | NORTHERN IRELAND ASSEMBLY
HOUSE OF COMMONS | EUROPEAN PARLIAMENT

In groups:
a) Copy the picture of the signposts above on a large sheet of paper.
b) Read statements 1–10 opposite, and decide which institution from the four above you think made this decision.
c) Record your answers beside the appropriate signpost.
d) Share your views with the rest of the class and adjust your answers if necessary.
e) Check your answers on page 90.
f) Refer to the table you created in Activity 1 of Topic 21. Use the space you left for a row for the issues about which each institution can make decisions.

1) Every household in a council area is given a recycling box.

2) The tax on petrol is increased in the UK because of the Budget.

3) The streetlights on a dark country road have been repaired.

4) Fur farming has been banned in Northern Ireland.

5) Rules have been made to limit the amount of cod fished in the Irish sea.

6) Funding has been refused for a local community festival.

7) The accident and emergency facilities in a local hospital have been closed.

8) Due to a terrorist threat in the UK a law has been passed extending the amount of time the police can question suspects.

9) A new law has been passed to define hate crimes in Northern Ireland.

10) Signs have been put up banning public drinking.

As you discovered in Activity 1 in Topic 21, the different political institutions make decisions on different types of issues. So, do you know which institution is responsible for which issues in general?

Activity 2 Heads and tails

Match the start of each of the sentences below to the correct ending. Write out the complete sentences to summarise what you have learned in this topic.

1) The Northern Ireland Assembly makes decisions about …

2) Local councils make decisions about …

3) The European Parliament makes decisions about …

4) The UK government makes decisions about …

a) … European-wide policies on trade, agriculture, etc.

b) … taxes, defence, etc.

c) … health, education, environment, culture, agriculture, etc. in Northern Ireland.

d) … waste and recycling services, leisure and community services, etc.

Local and Global Citizenship

23 WHY SHOULD I TAKE ACTION IN A DEMOCRACY?

Learning intentions

I am learning:
- about why people should take action in their society
- to speak persuasively about issues I care about.

In Topic 16 you learned about some of the features of living in a democracy: being able to make your views heard and taking responsible action if you feel your representatives are not listening to you. In Topics 21 and 22 you found out who represents you and the types of decision they can make. In the next two topics, you will select an issue about which you want to bring about change and plan to carry out an action project based on that issue.

Activity 1 Why should we take action?

a) Read the statement below from Oxfam:

'A global citizen is someone who knows how the world works, is outraged by injustice and who is both willing and enabled to take action to meet this global challenge.'

Oxfam

Oxfam is a development agency that seeks to influence the powerful to ensure that people in poverty can improve their lives and livelihoods and have a say in decisions that affect them.

It makes me angry when I see poverty in the world and governments not caring …

Something has to be done about people around the world suffering in wars …

Why do some children not have the same chances as I have?

Outraged citizen of the world

b) Create a spider diagram to answer the following questions:
- What type of global issues should 'outrage' the citizens of the world?
- What type of local issues should 'outrage' people in your local community?
- Why should they do something about these issues?
- Do you think global or local issues matter more? Why?

c) Write your own statement to explain why you think an effective citizen should want to take action in their local and global communities.

Now that you have generated a number of local and global issues that you think should outrage the citizens of the world and people in your community, the next activity will give you an opportunity to persuade others in your class to act on the one that you think is the most important.

Activity 2 Choosing an issue

In groups:

a) Compare all your spider diagrams from Activity 1. Together generate ideas for local and global issues you feel strongly about. You could use the sources below for ideas.

Trawl local and national newspapers

Search news websites or websites of NGOs

Watch the news or documentaries

b) Decide on one local issue and one global issue about which you would like to take action.

c) Design a poster to convince the rest of the class that they should take action on your issues. Carry out research so that you are better informed about your issues. Include images, facts and figures and even some ideas about what you could do and what you would hope to achieve.

d) Select one or two members of your group to make a 'pitch' to the rest of the class. You will have one minute to speak to your class about each issue. When all the issues have been pitched, display all your posters around the room.

e) Each member of the class has a total of ten votes to distribute between the issues they feel strongly about. Use sticky dots to represent your ten votes. You can give all ten votes to one issue, one vote to ten issues, or split the votes in any other way you wish across a number of issues. You decide – it's your vote!

f) When everyone has voted arrange the issues in rank order to select the one you want to take forward. Record the issue and state why your class has decided to take action on this.

24 HOW CAN WE CARRY OUT AN ACTION PROJECT?

Learning intentions

I am learning:
- ✓ to organise and take part in an action project
- ✓ to evaluate the skills I use and develop through taking part in an action project.

In Topic 23 you selected an issue you felt strongly about and decided to take action on it. This topic will help you to plan and carry out your action project. There are many ways in which you can plan your project. You could use the action planning template and questions from Topic 5 in the Personal Development section of this book. Activity 1 below uses a different approach to help you start thinking about the best way to take action on an issue.

Activity 1 Action project tree

As a class:
a) Look at the diagram of the tree. Make a copy of it without the labels on a very large sheet of paper.
b) Record the issue you want to take action on or the change that you want to see happen on the tree trunk.
c) Think about how you will know you have been successful. Record these outcomes as fruits on the tree.
d) Think about the types of actions you could take. Record these on the branches of the tree.

- Consider how NGOs (non-governmental organisations) bring about change.
- How could you use your local representatives?
- Could you involve the media?

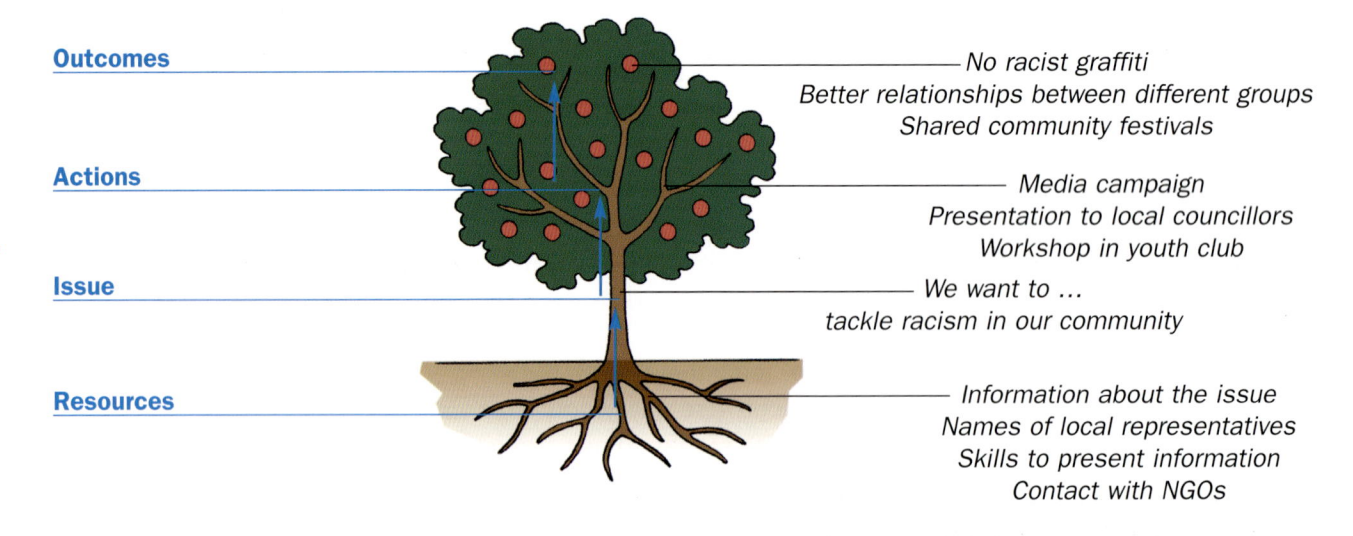

Outcomes
- No racist graffiti
- Better relationships between different groups
- Shared community festivals

Actions
- Media campaign
- Presentation to local councillors
- Workshop in youth club

Issue
- We want to … tackle racism in our community

Resources
- Information about the issue
- Names of local representatives
- Skills to present information
- Contact with NGOs

We are going to … organise a presentation to our local councillors to suggest ways in which we could improve relationships between different ethnic groups in our community.

Local and Global Citizenship

48

e) Think about the resources, skills and contacts you will need to make these actions happen. Record these on the roots of the tree.
f) Examine your tree and decide on specific and realistic actions you could take on your issue. Record these in a box under your tree.

Once you have planned your project, put it into action to see if you can effect change on your issue. To do this successfully you will need to be organised and communicate well to make sure everyone knows what they need to do.

Activity 2 Carrying out the action project

As a class:
a) Make a list of the all the jobs that need to be done and organise them into different committees. Assign pupils to each committee and give everyone a task to carry out.
b) Copy and complete a blank version of the table below for your action project as a record of your decisions.

Name of committee	Jobs	Pupils' names and tasks
Information committee	Gather information about the types of ethnic groups who contribute to our community and their experiences of living here	John – find out about the work of NGOs Lesley – media trawl Anne-Marie – interview local people
Policy committee	Gather details on the work of the local council and good contacts within it	June – search local council website Michael – interview local councillors

c) Use a planning sheet to help you keep track of your tasks.

My job(s)	What do I need?	How do I get it?	How can I get help?	Date to complete by

d) Meet regularly to discuss and review the progress of individual tasks, committees and the overall project.

Activity 3 Personal journal

When you have completed the project, remember to evaluate the overall process.

a) What did I learn about the issue?
b) Do I think the same about the issue now as I did at the start?
c) Was the action a success? How do I know this?
d) What would I do differently and why?
e) What skills did I use? What skills did I develop?

Local and Global Citizenship

49

25 WHAT ARE THE CHARACTERISTICS OF DEMOCRACY?

Learning intentions

I am learning:
- ✓ to understand the key features of democracy
- ✓ to learn about people who have taken action in non-democratic societies.

In Topics 23 and 24 you learned about how to develop an action project. Taking action is one way people can participate in a democracy. It is also something people can do to challenge undemocratic practices. As you learned in Topic 16, democracy is about much more than just voting. Democracy is about making sure that everyone is treated fairly and given equal opportunities in life, and ensuring that human rights are respected. There are many examples of individuals who have taken action for these reasons.

In the 1920s, Mohandas Karamchand (Mahatma) Gandhi used non-violent means of protest such as fasting and the boycott of British goods and British institutions to campaign against unjust laws and poor treatment of the Indian people.

On 1 December 1955 in Montgomery, Alabama, USA, Rosa Parks refused to obey bus driver James Blake's order to give up her seat to make room for a white passenger. Her action inspired many others to do the same.

Aung San Suu Kyi is a pro-democracy campaigner and leader of the Burmese National Democratic Party. She has organised peaceful rallies and non-violent protests around the world to try to bring an end to military repression in Burma.

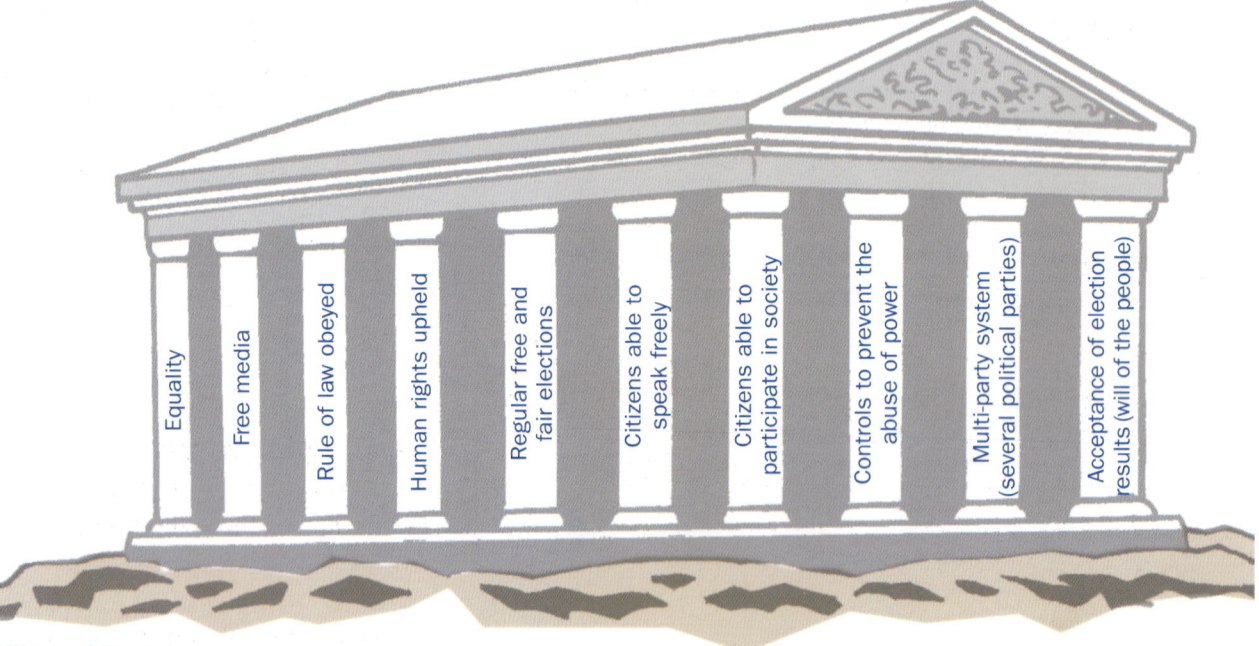

Pillars of Democracy

Pillars labelled: Equality; Free media; Rule of law obeyed; Human rights upheld; Regular free and fair elections; Citizens able to speak freely; Citizens able to participate in society; Controls to prevent the abuse of power; Multi-party system (several political parties); Acceptance of election results (will of the people)

Activity 1 What are the key features of democracy?

a) Read the extract on the opposite page about Pol Pot. Use the pillars of democracy diagram above to explain how Pol Pot's actions ignored and abused these important democratic beliefs.

'All foreigners were expelled, embassies closed, and any foreign economic or medical assistance was refused. The use of foreign languages was banned. Newspapers and television stations were shut down, radios and bicycles confiscated, and mail and telephone usage curtailed. Money was forbidden. All businesses were shuttered, religion banned, education halted, health care eliminated, and parental authority revoked. Cambodia was sealed off from the outside world.'

(Source: www.unitedhumanrights.org/Genocide/pol_pot.htm)

In groups:

b) Search newspapers and the internet for three other examples of situations where people are currently being denied at least one of the pillars of democracy. Share your findings with the rest of the class and explain what you have learned.

As mentioned above the media can be a target of undemocratic governments, who try to control what they say. However the media in democratic countries also have an important role in making people aware of human rights abuses.

Activity 2 What's the point?

a) The images below and right all make a point about democracy, or the lack of it.

- Write down the point you think the image is trying to make. Use the key features of democracy to help you.
- Which image do you think makes the most impact? Why?

In 1989 the world's media showed this image of a protester in Tiananmen Square, China

This cartoon refers to Robert Mugabe who became leader of Zimbabwe in 1980

This is an image of a monk protesting in 2008 against the Chinese occupation of Tibet

Activity 3 Personal journal

a) Why do you think it is important to defend and uphold the beliefs and characteristics of democracy?

b) What would our society be like if people didn't care about democratic principles?

c) What can individuals, society and governments in democratic countries do to promote democracy around the world?

In groups:

b) Carry out a media search for similar images, cartoons, headlines or pictures, which have something to say about the pillars of democracy. Look for examples that are local and global.

c) Display your work for the rest of the class in a collage and discuss what you think each other's work has to say. Which of the collages is the most powerful? Why?

Local and Global Citizenship

26 | WHAT IS THE ROLE OF HUMAN RIGHTS IN A DEMOCRACY?

Learning intentions
I am learning:
- how human rights set standards for governments
- about the need to balance and limit human rights in a democracy.

In Topic 25 you discovered that human rights are important in a democracy. In a democracy citizens should be able to enjoy (have the benefit of) their human rights freely. Governments are responsible for making sure this happens. But do governments always make sure their citizens enjoy their rights?

International human rights law is a set of laws that governments must keep. It is made up of various international human rights instruments, like the Universal Declaration of Human Rights (UDHR) and the United Nations Convention on the Rights of the Child (UNCRC). The governments of the countries that signed these instruments have promised to make sure their own laws do not breach (go against) these international laws.

Activity 1 — Can governments break the law?

In groups:

a) International human rights law is based on the UDHR. Make sure your group has access to a copy of this (you can get a simplified version at www.un.org/cyberschoolbus/humanrights/resources/plain.asp).

b) Look at each of the real laws below and discuss how they breached international human rights law by identifying the promises it breaks.

Law 1
Buddhists believe in reincarnation. This is a belief that when a person dies their soul comes back to Earth in another body or form. In September 2007, the Chinese government in Tibet made it illegal for Tibetan Buddhist teachers, including the Dalai Lama, the spiritual leader of Tibet, to be reincarnated without their permission.

Law 2
In 1949 the South African government made marriages between white people and people of other skin colour illegal.

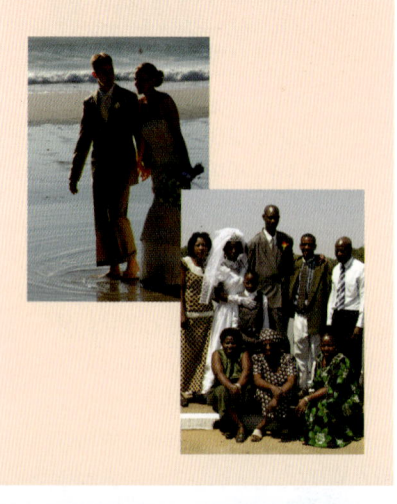

Law 3
In 1996 the Taliban government in Afghanistan banned women from working outside the home. Only a few female doctors and nurses were allowed to work in some hospitals.

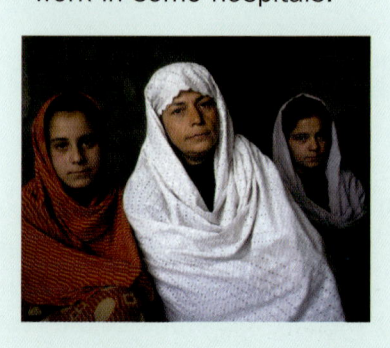

Local and Global Citizenship

As a class:

c) Discuss the following questions:

- Are laws always fair?
- Why are international human rights standards important for democracy?

Human rights are important for democracy because they set the standards for governments to live up to. But how can governments make sure that *everyone* enjoys their human rights equally in a democracy? What if one person's human rights conflict with another person's human rights? If everyone is to enjoy their human rights then most of them need to be balanced and limited in a democracy. If we want to enjoy our rights then others should be allowed to enjoy theirs.

Activity 2 Balancing human rights in a democracy

a) Think about the following statement: 'I have the right to freedom of expression so I can say whatever I want.'

- Do you agree or disagree with this?
- Which human rights from the UDHR does this need to be balanced against? That is, which rights might other people be deprived of if you enjoy this human right fully?
- How should this right be limited or restricted?

b) Copy the table below to record your discussion. Complete it for all the human rights listed. One has been completed as an example.

Human right	Should be limited if …	Needs to be balanced against …
Right to a peaceful public protest	The protest stops people from leaving their home or interrupts their family life	Right to privacy Right to freedom of movement
Freedom of expression		
Right to privacy		
Freedom of religion		
Freedom of movement from country to country		

The only human rights that are absolute (or unconditional) and can never be limited are freedom from slavery and from torture.

27 WHY DO WE NEED LAWS IN A DEMOCRACY?

Learning intentions

I am learning:
- ✓ about the purpose of laws
- ✓ to distinguish between examples of civil and criminal law.

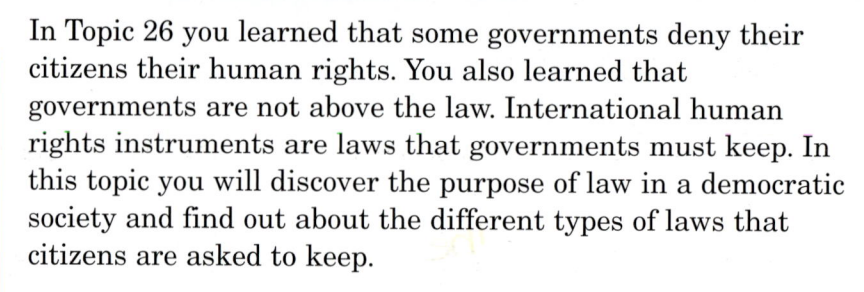

In Topic 26 you learned that some governments deny their citizens their human rights. You also learned that governments are not above the law. International human rights instruments are laws that governments must keep. In this topic you will discover the purpose of law in a democratic society and find out about the different types of laws that citizens are asked to keep.

💡 Activity 1 Images of the law

a) Look at the images on the left and use them, your own ideas and information from previous topics to generate a list of terms or phrases associated with the word 'law'. Try to categorise these into the following groups:

- people involved in the law
- institutions connected with the law (making law, enforcing law)
- examples of laws.

b) As a class, discuss the following questions:

- Where have your ideas about the law come from?
- How have your ideas about the law been shaped by what you have seen, read and experienced?
- Do you feel you have a fair and balanced view of what the law is about?
- Why do you think we need laws?

Sometimes our understanding of what is meant by the law is quite limited. We often just associate the law with crime and punishment. This is called 'criminal law'. However, the law also covers issues such as family life and business. This is called 'civil law'. The law serves a very important function in a democratic society. People in a democratic society must keep laws for the safety of others and to ensure we all behave in a socially responsible way.

Criminal law
These laws cover behaviour that is forbidden by the government because it threatens, harms or otherwise endangers the safety and welfare of the public.

Civil law
These laws cover issues that are not covered by criminal law. It usually refers to the settlement of disputes between individuals, organisations or groups.

Activity 2 — What type of law?

Look at the examples below and decide if they are covered by either civil or criminal law.

1) Shoplifting
2) Drink-driving 
3) Adopting a child 
4) Being given a licence to sell alcohol 
5) Under age drinking 
6) A personal injury claim 
7) Divorce 
8) Disorderly behaviour 
9) Murder 
10) Marriage or civil partnerships 

Activity 3 — Why have laws?

Complete the following sentences using the word bank to summarise what you have learned about the purpose of law.

Word bank
governments   protected   punishment   responsible
democratic   legal   disputes   human

Laws exist in a _____ society to make sure that people are _____ from harm and behave in a socially _____ way. They also state the types of _____ that can be given out if people break the law. Laws also help people to settle _____ and make _____ arrangements for families or businesses. Even _____ are not above the law. They must protect the _____ rights of their citizens.

If you want to find out about laws that directly affect you as a young person then visit the Children's Law Centre website:
www.childrenslawcentre.org

Local and Global Citizenship

28 HOW DO BREACHES OF THE LAW AFFECT THE COMMUNITY?

Learning intentions

I am learning:
- to explain how crime affects individuals and their communities
- to evaluate a range of explanations for why people commit crimes.

In Topic 27 you learned that the law exists to make sure that society is protected from harm and that people behave in a socially responsible way. In this topic, you will explore the effects on the community if someone commits a crime and breaks the law.

Activity 1 The thin end of the wedge

In groups:

a) Make a large copy of the wedge diagram below (just copy the shape of the wedge, not the words or the thought bubbles).

b) Choose one of the crimes described opposite (1–6) and write it in the first section of the wedge (make sure each group chooses a different crime!).

c) Complete the wedge diagram to explore the effects of this crime on the community. Use the thought bubbles as prompts to help you.

As a class:

d) Examine the completed wedge diagrams for each different crime. Compare and contrast the effects of these crimes.

- What do they have in common?
- When the law is broken, who is affected?
- How does crime affect individuals?
- How does it affect their families?
- How does crime affect the community?

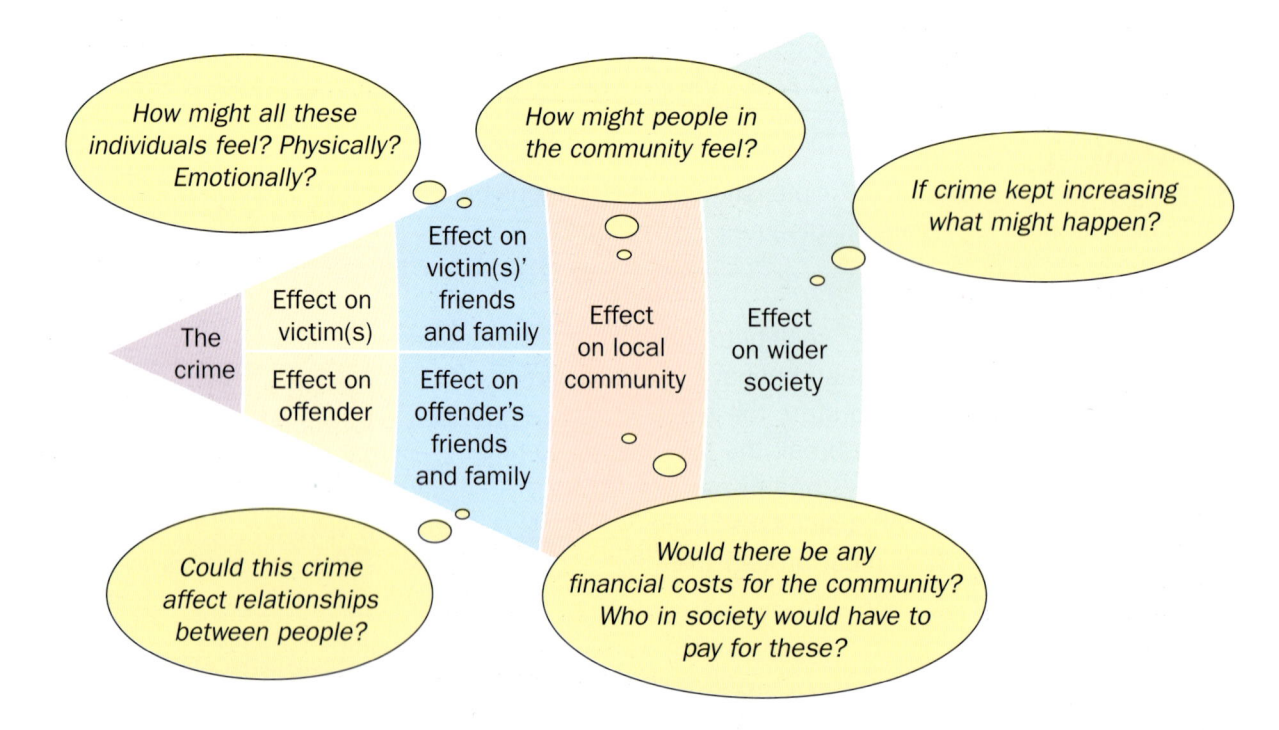

How might all these individuals feel? Physically? Emotionally?

How might people in the community feel?

If crime kept increasing what might happen?

The crime → Effect on victim(s) / Effect on offender → Effect on victim(s)' friends and family / Effect on offender's friends and family → Effect on local community → Effect on wider society

Could this crime affect relationships between people?

Would there be any financial costs for the community? Who in society would have to pay for these?

Local and Global Citizenship

56

1) **There is an armed robbery in a local post office.**

2) **A community centre is vandalised.**

3) **A young women has her handbag stolen in the street.**

4) **Illegal drugs are being sold in a local club.**

5) **A classroom is set on fire in a local primary school.**

6) **A family have their car stolen.**

Since crimes cause so much harm to society it is useful to step back and think about why people commit crimes and how we could prevent this from happening. Experts in crime (called criminologists) do not always agree on these issues. There are several different viewpoints.

Activity 2 Why do people commit crime?

In groups:
a) Read each viewpoint below and discuss whether you agree or disagree with the experts. You may wish to use examples to support your arguments (for example from newspapers or TV).
b) For each viewpoint, discuss what you think the experts would suggest should be done to prevent people from committing crimes? For example, one suggestion for viewpoint 1 might be to provide people in disadvantaged areas with a better education.

Activity 3
Personal journal

Write down your own view on why people commit crime and the steps that you think could be taken by individuals, society and government to prevent crimes.

Viewpoint 1

Most experts think people commit crime because of the **social or economic conditions** they live in. Perhaps they had a difficult home life or poor education. Maybe because of a poor education they didn't get any qualifications or develop any skills and perhaps because of this cannot find employment. Maybe they are living in poverty and turn to crime because they can see no other way out of their situation.

Viewpoint 2

Many experts think if people have **poor role models** or associate with criminals then they are more likely to commit crimes themselves. They might see criminals in their area living a 'good life' and being able to afford designer clothes, expensive cars and so on. They might even be influenced by the images of crime on TV or in films. Once they are caught up in this world they might then find it hard to get out of it. If they end up in prison with criminals it might just encourage them more.

Viewpoint 3

A few experts think that some people are just '**born bad**' and make a personal choice to commit crimes because they want to. These experts do not think that the ideas expressed in viewpoints 1 and 2 have any bearon why people commit crime.

Local and Global Citizenship

29 HOW CAN LAWS BE ENFORCED?

Learning intentions

I am learning:
- about how laws are enforced in Northern Ireland
- the types of punishments given for different crimes.

In Topic 28 you explored how the community is affected when laws are broken and also suggested some ways to prevent crime happening. In this topic you will consider some of the ways people can be made answerable for the crimes they have committed.

The Criminal Justice System in Northern Ireland is responsible for investigating crimes, finding the people who have committed the crimes and bringing those people to justice. You can find out more from the website www.cjsni.gov.uk. There are many different parts of this system and each has its own role.

Activity 1 The Criminal Justice System

a) Match each part of the Criminal Justice System in the jigsaw below to its function (or job).

A Decide whether someone should be prosecuted for a crime and bring the case to court.

B Provide information to the court about offenders and try to prevent reoffending.

C Look after the needs of young offenders and help them turn away from crime.

1. Police Service of Northern Ireland
2. Northern Ireland Court Service
3. Northern Ireland Prison Service
4. Public Prosecution Service
5. Probation Board for Northern Ireland
6. Youth Justice Agency

D Look after offenders who are given a prison sentence.

E Look after the running of the courts.

F Investigate crimes, gather evidence and charge offenders.

b) Choose a part of the Criminal Justice System that interests you and find out more about what it does. You could visit its website or organise a guest speaker to learn about its role.

c) There are two more organisations which are not part of the Criminal Justice System, but do play an important role. Find out what they do:

- the Office of the Police Ombudsman
- the Criminal Justice Inspectorate.

If someone is convicted of a crime by a court of law in Northern Ireland, the judge or the magistrate decides on the type of punishment or sentence that should be given. There are many different ways in which offenders can be made answerable for the harm that they have done.

Activity 2 Group project: 'crime and punishment'

In groups of six:
a) Allocate one of the following topics to each member of your group. This is your 'home group'.

1) Community Service Orders for adults in Northern Ireland	2) Sentences for young people in Northern Ireland	3) Restorative justice in communities across the world	4) The history of crime and punishment	5) The death penalty	6) Prison sentences for adults in Northern Ireland

b) Form new groups: everyone in the class who has been allocated topic 1 should group together, all the 2s group together, all the 3s, and so on. These new groups are your 'expert groups'.

c) Research the topic you have been given in your expert group.

- Find out as much information as possible, using the internet, the library, even your teacher as a resource!
- Don't just find out facts; try to evaluate the different approaches to punishment, the pros and cons, people's views on the issues, and so on.
- Make sure each member of the group has a copy of all the information gathered.

d) Return to your home group and together produce a display on the theme 'crime and punishment'.

- Include information from all the experts in your group.
- Agree on a final statement from your home group about what you think is the best way to deal with people who commit crimes.

30 WHAT HAVE I LEARNED ABOUT CITIZENSHIP?

Learning intentions

I am learning:
- ✓ to reflect on the knowledge I have gained and skills I have developed during citizenship topics
- ✓ to explain what is meant by 'citizenship'.

In Book 1 and Book 2 you learned that Local and Global Citizenship is about discovering how you can get involved in the issues that affect the communities you belong to; for example, your school, your local area, your town, your country and the wider world. You also learned that to do this you need to develop your knowledge about key issues affecting society and develop skills to help you play an effective and active part in today's world. In this topic you will reflect on what you have learned about citizenship through all the activities you have completed.

Activity 1 The citizenship umbrella

a) Make a large copy of the drawing of the umbrella (without the labels).

b) Think of all the topics and issues you have covered as you have explored all the themes of Local and Global Citizenship (some are shown in the photos below).

Human rights and social responsibility

Diversity and inclusion

Equality and social justice

Democracy and active participation

c) Record on raindrops some of the problems or negative issues you have learned about.

d) Now think about the solutions to these problems or positive things you have learned about. Record these on the individual sections of the open umbrella.

e) Now think about the skills you have developed. Record these on the handle of the umbrella.

f) Think about the following questions and record your thoughts under the umbrella:

- Who would you invite underneath your umbrella?
- What groups of people should be protected by your citizenship umbrella?
- Who should help you hold up the umbrella?

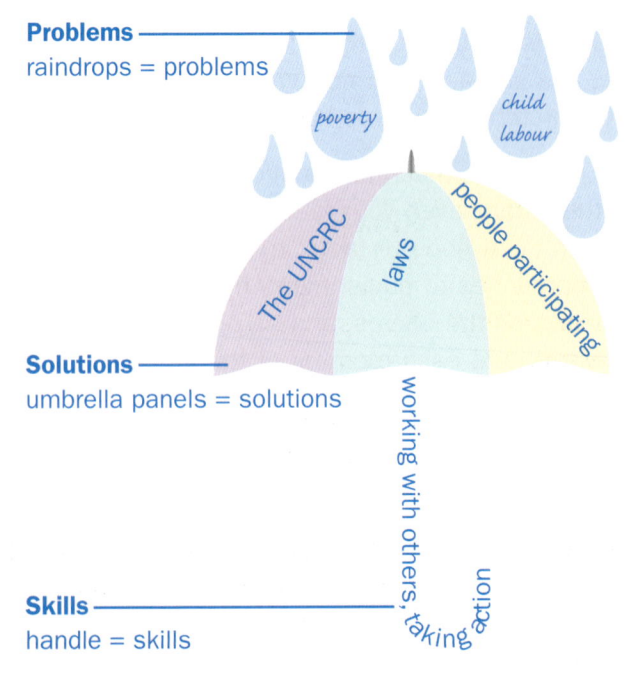

Problems — raindrops = problems

poverty, *child labour*

Solutions — umbrella panels = solutions

The UNCRC, *laws*, *people participating*

Skills — handle = skills

working with others, taking action

Local and Global Citizenship

60

Activity 2 Being a citizen

The pictures on the right show three ways of thinking about 'citizenship'.

In groups:

a) Discuss the following questions:

- Which description do you think captures the most important features of 'citizenship'? Why?
- Do you think any of the descriptions give a complete picture of what citizenship is about? If so, how? If not, why not?

b) Together agree a single definition of 'citizenship'. Share this with the rest of the class and try to arrive at a whole-class definition.

1) Citizenship is about your relationship with those in authority above you. It's about expecting your government to look after its citizens and to protect their rights.

2) Citizenship is about your relationships with the communities you belong to locally and globally. It's about giving something back to those communities.

3) Citizenship is just about your nationality – the country you belong to.

Activity 3 Personal journal

What you learn in Local and Global Citizenship can be summed up in terms of what you know, how you feel, and what you would like to do. You may remember that at the end of your citizenship topics in Book 1 and Book 2 you completed a reflection on these ideas. The grid gives you an example of how someone might reflect on their learning throughout their citizenship topics. Copy a blank version of the table below and complete it for your own learning.

	Knowing	Feeling	Doing
Before exploring Local and Global Citizenship …	I didn't really know much about the issues that affect my society.	I didn't care that much about global issues.	I had never really told anyone my views on issues.
Now …	I know about things like poverty, how to challenge racism and who represents me.	I feel quite strongly about human rights abuses in countries like China.	I am confident talking about what I think – even to politicians!
I would like to …	Find out more about how young people can be encouraged away from crime.	Believe I could really make a difference.	Get more involved in my community.

31 | HOW DO I MAKE DECISIONS?

Learning intentions

I am learning:
- ✓ to recognise who influences my decisions
- ✓ different strategies to help me make the right decisions.

How do you make decisions?

How you make choices or decisions will depend largely on what that decision is and how important the outcome is to you. You will probably put more thought into who you will marry than who you will sit beside in French. As a young child almost all your decisions were influenced or even made by your parents: where you went, what you wore, what time you went to bed, and so on. As you have got older they have let you make more decisions without them. So what do you base these decisions on?

In Book 1 Topic 15 and Topic 37 you thought about some of the people and things that might influence your decisions. Look at the pictures below to remind you. Can you suggest any other influences?

Activity 1
Decisions, decisions

In groups:
a) List different ways to make decisions including the examples on the right.
b) As a class agree on a list of the main strategies used. Stick up a sign for each one at a different point in the room.
c) Consider the first of the problems shown in the pictures on page 63. Agree in your group which you think is the best way to make the decision. Send one person from your group to stand at the appropriate sign. Are all the groups in agreement? Repeat the exercise for the other problems.

As well as being influenced by others we use different strategies to make different decisions. For example:

- where to go on Saturday night – make a list of pros and cons
- what to order from the Chinese – most popular vote among friends
- who bats first in rounders – toss a coin.

1)
2)
3)
4)
5)
6)

In Year 10 your main decision in school will be which subjects to choose for GCSE. Your goal is to make the best choice for you. To make the right decision you need to consider your options and gather information to help you make an informed decision. This is not the time to make a random decision or just follow the crowd. In the next few topics you will carry out the actions needed to reach this goal.

Activity 2 Personal journal

In both Book 1 (Topic 36) and Book 2 (Topic 30) you used the personal career planning model to help you set out steps to reach a goal. The flowchart shows some targets and actions you could complete to move towards your goal of choosing your GCSE subjects.

a) Copy the flowchart into your journal. Add to or replace the steps with any others you think are more appropriate.

b) Consider which of the actions you can complete now. Make a note of the information you already have.

- What do you still need to find out?
- What will your next action be?

Goal – I want to choose the best GCSE subjects for me.

↑

Find out what each subject is like at GCSE or about any new subjects.

↑

Check which subjects I might need for further study or a particular job.

↑

List the subjects I most enjoy and the ones I am best at.

↑

Find out which subjects I have to choose from.

↑

I am in Year 10 and need to choose my GCSEs.

Education for Employability

63

32 WHERE CAN I GET HELP?

Learning intentions

I am learning:
- to identify the people who can help me
- to ask appropriate questions
- what other sources of information are available in my school.

Over the next couple of months as you prepare to make your GCSE choices you will need to gather information to help you make the right decision. You will also have questions that need answering. In Topic 15 you learned about accessing help in your community. In this topic, you will focus on finding out where to get help with choosing your GCSE subjects.

Your school will probably have software programs to provide you with information about careers, jobs and courses and to guide you on how your skills and qualities can best be used. Newspapers, magazines and the internet also allow you access to lots of useful information. But one of the best sources of information is people!

People who can help you

Activity 1 Who can answer my questions?

Individually:

a) Look at the diagram above of people who can help you. Make a list of the actual names of these people around you.

As a class:

b) Identify the best person or group of people to answer the following questions. You may not all agree on the same answer for all the questions.

- Which subjects must I continue to study next year?
- Which subjects can I choose from?
- Could I cope with this GCSE course?
- In what way is the GCSE different to KS3?
- How much time will I need to spend on homework and coursework at home?
- Is the GCSE enjoyable?
- Will this subject be useful to me?
- I have never studied this before: what is it about?

c) Add any other questions you consider important. Think about who could answer those questions for you.

Activity 2 Tell me more

As a class:
a) Arrange a time to invite some Year 12 pupils into your classroom to tell you about their experiences. Try to invite a range of people studying different subjects.

In groups:
b) In the lesson before the interviews, list some questions you think would be appropriate. Try to cover everything you want to find out about what it is like to study all the different subjects available.

In school you most likely have a career suite or office where information is available about different jobs and courses at colleges and universities. Your school will also have access to careers software packages such as Pathfinder, Odyssey and CID, which help to match suitable jobs to your skills, interests and abilities based on your answers to various questions. There are also many useful websites on the internet, including:

- www.careersserviceni.com
- www.careers-gateway.co.uk
- www.careersadvice.direct.gov.uk

Careers advice is available from your school's careers suite or office

Activity 3 Search the suite

In groups:
a) Visit the career suite or office in the school, making a note of all the different ways you can access information.
b) Make a poster or design a leaflet to show pupils using the career suite the different ways in which they can carry out research and when they can do this.
c) Pass your posters and leaflets to the Head of Careers to be used to help others.

Careers advice is available on the internet or from software programs

You will get the opportunity to see how effective your guidance has been over the next few topics as you start to look at jobs you might do and find out more about them.

33 HOW DO I START TO CHOOSE A CAREER?

Learning intentions

I am learning:
- to identify the type of work I enjoy
- to evaluate my skills and qualities
- to investigate my job options.

Before you can make an informed decision about your GCSEs you need to give some thought to the type of work you may end up doing. You are not expected to choose a specific career at this stage, although you may have definite ideas already. However, it is wise to consider the area you might end up working in, as certain jobs require certain qualifications at GCSE. So, how do you begin to find out which job might suit you? One way is to consider the activities you are good at and enjoy already.

Judy's story

Judy has two sisters, but when they were all living at home her bedroom was the only one kept tidy. She hated her sisters borrowing things and not putting them back in the proper place. When it came to school work she was always on time with her homework and never in a panic revising for exams. As well as this, she still managed to play hockey three times a week and chaired the school fundraising committee in Year 13. Judy has now got a very responsible job as a production manager in a large manufacturing firm in Northern Ireland and she loves her work.

Activity 1 School matters

As a class:

- Discuss what clues there were in Judy's school life as to the type of job she would enjoy and succeed at.
- What skills and qualities did she develop at school that are useful to her now?

You all work at school already and many of you will also do jobs around your house or activities outside school. Thinking about the things you like doing might give you a clue to what career you would enjoy.

Education for Employability

66

Activity 2 Clues to the future

Individually:
a) Make a list of the tasks you do at home.
b) Add any activities you do or hobbies you have.
c) Use one colour to circle or highlight the things you most enjoy. Use a different colour to circle or highlight the things you hate having to do.
d) Review your list to see what it says about you.

- Is there any pattern to the activities you most enjoy?
- What qualities and skills do you think your list suggests you have?

Setting the table
Tidying my room
Looking after my younger sister
Shopping
Word-processing my homework
Researching on the internet
Organising my file
Playing on the football team
Helping out at scout group

Activity 3 Twenty-first century help

Use a software package or website to help you determine your qualities and skills. It might suggest interesting jobs you have never considered or even heard of.

- Do you think you would enjoy the jobs suggested for you?
- How accurate do you think the results are?
- Do think the results should be used with caution? If so, why?

Resources
Pathfinder, Odyssey and CID are all available through C2kni.
www.bbc.co.uk/northernireland/schools
www.careersadvice.direct.gov.uk

Activity 4 Career hunting

In pairs:
a) Interview your partner about their results from Activity 3. Find out as much as you can about their subject and career interests.
b) Design a one-page brochure, rather like that for selling a house, to promote your partner.

- If you have access to a digital camera, include a photo.
- State the qualities and skills they have.
- Suggest jobs they would be suitable for.

c) Display the brochures around your classroom.

Education for Employability

67

34 WHAT ARE MY 'OPTIONS'?

Learning intentions

I am learning:
- why some subjects are so important
- which subjects suit my learning style.

Before you can make any definite decisions about what you study in KS4, you need to know what your options are. What subjects can you drop? Are there new subjects you can study? Can you only do GCSEs? Is your choice completely open?

Hopefully this will have been explained to you already; if not you will need to invite the person in charge of the curriculum into your class to talk to you.

Regardless of your preferences some subjects are just too important to leave behind completely, but can you see why?

Activity 1 You're dropped

School funding for KS4 has been greatly reduced. Your school needs to take drastic action and make cuts in one department.

In groups:

You will be assigned one of the following departments: Maths, English, Science, Modern Foreign Languages, IT, Home Economics. Your task is to fight for your department's survival.

a) On a flipchart list reasons why you think your subject is important for pupils aged 14 to 16.

- Consider how it will help them to be more employable.
- How will it affect their personal development?
- List any skills and qualities it might develop.

b) Present your argument to the rest of the class.
c) Take a class vote on which subject should be dropped.

Remember, just because your class decides to drop a certain subject does not mean it is not important. Another class may reach a completely different decision. All subjects offer so much more than just an exam qualification. Your school will require you to carry on with the subjects they consider to be necessary for your future success. Make a note of these subjects in your personal journal.

In most cases you will have some choices to make about the subjects you study over the next two years. In many cases jobs require a good level of education rather than exams in particular subjects. Even jobs that do have specific requirements will only dictate a small number of your subject choices. It is up to you to choose the rest, but how?

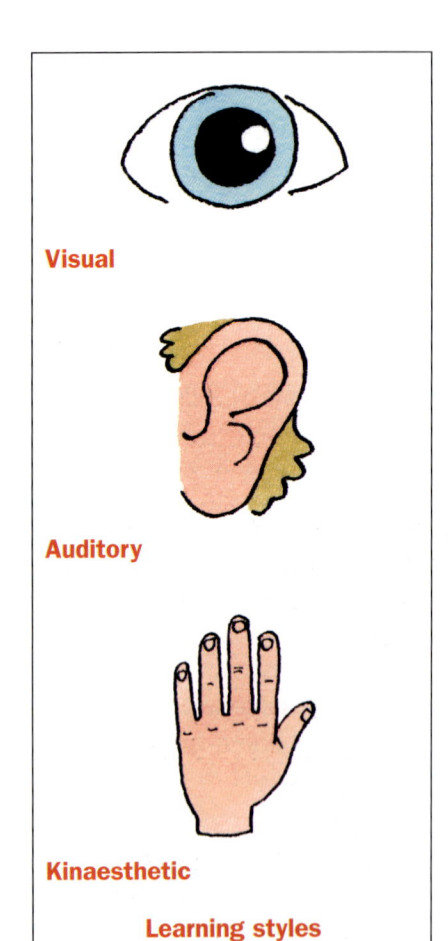

Visual

Auditory

Kinaesthetic

Learning styles

Learning styles and environments

Different subjects at school often require you to learn in a certain way, so choosing a subject that matches your preferred learning style should mean you are more comfortable studying it and therefore perform better. If you are unsure about your preferred learning style, refer back to Topic 9 in Book 1 or use the quiz at www.usd.edu/trio/tut/ts/style.html to remind you what each means.

Something else that may affect how much you enjoy a subject, and therefore how well you do, is the learning environment. Do you learn better when you work mainly alone (intrapersonal environment) or when you often work in groups, sharing ideas and information (interpersonal environment)?

Intrapersonal environment

Interpersonal environment

Activity 2 Subjects under the spotlight

In groups:
Copy and complete the table below for all the subjects you can choose from at your school. Ask your subject teachers for ideas to complete the last column.

Subject	Learning style (V or A or K)	Learning environment (Intra- or interpersonal)	Jobs it is useful for
Biology			
French			
Technology			

Activity 3
Personal journal

Reflect on what you have discovered during this topic to see if your choices are any clearer.
a) Which subjects must you continue with?
b) Which of the subjects you can choose from do you enjoy?
c) Do you think you will work harder and do better at subjects you like?
d) Are there any you don't like but feel strongly that you should continue with?

Education for Employability

35 WHICH SUBJECTS SHOULD I STUDY?

Learning intentions

I am learning:
- ✓ to identify how subjects studied can help me develop essential work skills
- ✓ to complete a job study and decide how well it matches my skills and interests.

In Topics 33 and 34, you learned that in addition to your skills, personal qualities, interests, likes and dislikes, the subjects you choose to study for GCSE may impact on your ultimate career. For example, Maths and English at GCSE are essential for the majority of jobs. Access to most medical, dental and veterinary courses at university requires Chemistry at A level.

This topic will help you to recognise which subjects will enable you to develop the skills required for the type of job you would like to gain in future. You will also identify which, if any, subjects are essential or useful for entry to specific jobs.

Activity 1 Essential skills for work

In groups:

a) Select one of the job titles below and, using the skills wheel, list all the skills that you feel are essential to do that job. Include other skills you think of that are not on the wheel.

Doctor  **Aerobics instructor**  **Chef**  **Social worker**

Skills wheel:
- Time keeping
- Oral communication
- Motivational skills
- Written communication
- Practical skills
- Decision-making skills
- Organisational skills
- Problem-solving skills
- Initiative
- Creative skills
- People skills
- Team skills
- ICT skills
- Numeracy

Detective  **Receptionist**

Tour guide  **Bricklayer**  **Teacher**  **Estate agent**

b) Rank the skills in order from the most to least essential with most essential as number 1.

c) As a class, agree a common list of up to ten essential skills, based on your rankings.

Education for Employability

Essential skill	Subjects	Activity
Written communication	English	Writing about lots of different things in different formats, e.g. letters, reports

d) Assign one of the essential skills to each group to identify ways in which particular subjects can help develop this skill. An example is given in the table above.

e) Add any other activities suggested by the class to your list.

f) Choose a subject and design a poster to show how that subject can support the development of essential skills for work. Display the posters in the classroom.

Now you have identified some of the skills you may need in your career, you can start to match these to jobs you are interested in.

Job title:

Job details:	What the job involves:	Skills:
Hours:	Entry requirements: Age:	Essential subjects:
Pay:	Exam level:	Useful subjects:

Job family: identify which job family the job belongs to (circle as appropriate)

Practical   Investigative   Artistic
Social   Organisational   Enterprising

A job study

Activity 2 Job study

a) Select a job that interests you and you feel you might be good at. Refer to your job match list from Topic 33, Activity 3, for ideas.

b) Copy and complete the job study above for your chosen job by researching it using information from JED (the Job Explorer Database), Odyssey or www.careerserviceni.com.

c) Compile a list of all the subjects identified as essential or useful.

- Why are these subjects regarded as important?
- What other subjects may be of value?

d) Discuss the information for jobs from different job families.

Activity 3 Personal journal

Consider your personal skills, likes and dislikes. Compare these to your job study and answer the following questions in order to assess your suitability for the job.

a) Which of the skills required for the job do you have?

b) Which of the essential/helpful subjects identified do you intend to study?

c) Do you feel you will be able to achieve the qualifications necessary to gain this job?

d) Why do you think the job might/might not be for you?

36 WHAT TYPES OF JOBS ARE IN DEMAND?

Learning intentions
I am learning:
- ✓ about employment trends
- ✓ to design interview questions and carry out an interview
- ✓ to present a job profile.

Knowledge of employment trends in Northern Ireland may be of some help to you as you seek to choose a career direction. You have already learned about the negative impact globalisation and new technologies can have on businesses and employment opportunities in Northern Ireland in Book 1, Topics 40, 41 and 42. Newspapers are littered with stories about jobs moving to places like India and China. However, it's not all bad news. The 'peace dividend' has resulted in greater numbers of tourists visiting Northern Ireland which has created considerable growth in the tourism, hospitality, catering and creative sectors. In addition, the aging population means an increase in health care services is needed, while growing interest in fitness has caused an expansion of opportunities in the leisure industry.

In this topic you will find out more about these growth industries by interviewing people who work in the different sectors. First you will need to plan and design a questionnaire.

Tourism

Hospitality

Catering

ICT

Leisure

Health care

Creative

Activity 1 Designing a questionnaire

In groups:
a) Choose a sector from the growth industries (use the photos above to give you ideas).
b) Brainstorm to make a list of all the questions you might ask a person in order to find out about the job they do. These can include questions about:

- the hours they work
- the duties they perform
- what they like about their job
- what skills they need.

Education for Employability

72

c) Choose the ten best questions. Select the questions that will give you the most information. Write these questions down in the order that you will ask them.
d) Design the layout for the questionnaire leaving space for the answers to your questions. Remember to include some instructions for the interviewee to explain what you are trying to find out.

Once you have designed your questionnaire, you will need to find a target for your interview. Choose someone who works in one of the employment growth sectors or someone who does a job in another sector that particularly interests you.

Activity 2 Conducting the interview

In pairs:
a) Discuss the jobs that members of your family and friends do. Identify any people who work in the employment growth areas.
b) Choose one or more people to interview.
c) With your teacher's help, arrange to carry out an interview with your person of choice either face to face, by telephone or email.
d) Use your questionnaire to note down the answers to your questions. It may be helpful to record your interview, but remember to ask permission first.

Activity 3 Creating a job profile

In groups:
a) Share the results of your interview with other pairs who interviewed people in the same job sector.
b) Discuss what you have found out and use the information to create a job profile for that sector.
c) Present your job profile to the class. Highlight:

- the most common aspects amongst the different job roles you interviewed
- what you found most interesting
- anything unexpected that you learned.

A Day in the Life ... Firefighter

Seáinin Daykin   Position: Firefighter, Blue Watch, Cadogan Fire Station

What attracted you to a career in Northern Ireland Fire & Rescue Service?
The main attraction for me was that a career as a firefighter was very different from any other job that I had researched while I was still at school. I was instantly attracted to this job as I could help people, provide a vital service and learn new skills.

What do you enjoy most about working for Northern Ireland Fire & Rescue Service?
I enjoy going into the community and visiting schools and talking to people about fire safety and how they can protect themselves. I enjoy the shifts that we work as it's not routine 9–5 every day.

Outline what a typical day is like for you?
No two shifts are ever the same, and we never know what we might be faced with when responding to an emergency call. In a 'normal' day we could attend a house fire, a road traffic collision, a flooding incident or even a water rescue incident.

Do you feel you have developed any additional skills/qualities working as a firefighter?
I have developed myself and been developed in areas of teamwork, understanding, community relations, dignity and integrity. These are only a few of the qualities that are required to fulfil the role of a competent firefighter.

Example of a questionnaire

Source: www.nifrs.org/careers.php

37 WHAT DO PEOPLE GAIN FROM WORK?

Learning intentions

I am learning:
- about the types of things that motivate people to work
- to identify what factors will motivate me.

Why do people work? Most people work because they need to earn money in order to live. However, many people choose the work they do because of the personal enjoyment they gain from their job. This is called 'job satisfaction'.

It's never the same two days in a row!

I really feel appreciated.

I just like the work, even the long hours don't bother me.

So, what is job satisfaction? Job satisfaction describes how content an individual is with his or her job – possibly through the personal pleasure gained from a job well done, from knowing that what they do is appreciated by others, or from being able to buy what they want with the wages earned.

People who enjoy what they are doing usually do it well. Therefore, employers are keen to have employees who are motivated and have high levels of job satisfaction. Motivated employees help to create a good working atmosphere for all. They are generally more positive towards clients and customers and they often bring better results, whether in a business or a non-profit organisation.

I love helping people. I would do it even if I were not paid.

However, it can be difficult for employers to know how to give their employees greater job satisfaction as motivation means different things to different people. People may be motivated by money, success, enjoyment, security, recognition or feeling they are doing good for others. These are called 'motivational factors' and can be organised under five headings.

Self-fulfilment – personal satisfaction, for instance feeling you are doing something interesting and worthwhile

Security – a secure and safe job that does not change

Material comforts – the things your wages can buy, for instance a car or holidays

Power – being in charge; gaining personal recognition and status

Relationships – enjoying being with the people you work with; having self-respect

Motivational factors based on Maslow's pyramid of need

Activity 1 Sorting motivational factors

In groups:
a) On a large sheet of paper, draw a table with five columns. Write one of the five motivational factor headings at the top of each column.
b) Take turns to copy one of the motivational factors below onto a sticky note or small piece of paper. Place the motivational factor under one of the headings and explain why you think it fits there.
c) The rest of the group decide if they agree.

Look after people	Work as part of a team	Be my own boss	Manage other people	Long summer holidays	Annual bonus payments
Decide how and when to do work	Stay in the same job for working life	Make important decisions	Have fun with my colleagues	Be offered new opportunities	Receive recognition for my work
Get overtime payments	Be respected by fellow workers	Good promotion prospects	Long-term prospects are good	Travel and stay in the best hotels	Do interesting work
Receive on-the-job training	Have a high level of responsibility	Get a new company car each year	Deal directly with customers	Receive good wages	Have good work colleagues

Activity 2 Matching motivational factors to jobs

In groups:
List the top six motivating factors for each of the jobs below.

- Are they the same?
- Are they different?
- Why do you think they are similar or different?

Actor Nurse Judge University lecturer

Travel agent Self-employed consultant Painter and decorator Sales manager

Activity 3 Personal journal

It is important that you can identify what motivates you as this will help you select the types of job that are most suitable for you. The more motivated you are in work, the greater job satisfaction you will have.

a) List the top six factors that you think will be important to you in choosing a future job.
b) Which of the factors don't motivate you?
c) Compare these with what you have already found out about any jobs that interest you.

Education for Employability

38 HOW CAN I MAKE MYSELF MORE EMPLOYABLE?

Learning intentions

I am learning:
- about what 'employability' means to employers
- to identify and develop my employability skills
- to develop a personal profile.

What employers want

A survey of employers carried out by the Confederation of British Industry (CBI) identified the key to a person's employability as 'a set of attributes, skills and knowledge'. Along with a positive attitude to life and work, these skills ensure that employees are effective in the workplace.

Activity 1 Developing employability skills

Individually:

a) Copy and complete the table below. Consider each skill area. Think of as many examples as you can and rate yourself as good, fair or poor in each skill area.

In pairs:

b) Suggest ideas to help you develop each skill area. Use the examples to help you.

c) Identify two areas you want to focus on and plan some actions to help you improve these skills.

Skill area	Examples	How good am I in this skill area?	How to demonstrate/develop this skill
Self-management	Time keeping, meeting deadlines		Setting an alarm to remind yourself to do something
Team skills	Working with others to achieve a common goal		Becoming a class representative on the school council
Communication and literacy	Reading and preparing a variety of written materials, using oral communication for a range of purposes in a variety of situations		Making presentations in class
ICT skills	Using the internet, emails, databases, spreadsheets, multimedia presentations, word-processing		Completing homework assignments using appropriate software
Numeracy	Counting, calculating measuring, weighing, handling data		Planning a budget and managing your money
Problem solving skills	Dealing with the unexpected		Participating in active learning
Business and customer awareness	Learning about businesses, customer service		Work experience placements

It is important that you develop a good knowledge and understanding of yourself and your personal strengths and weaknesses. This will help you begin to identify the type of career you wish to pursue in future. This knowledge may affect your GCSE subject choices and can motivate you in your school work if you know you need specific skills to gain the job you want.

Activity 2 My personal profile

Create your own personal profile.
a) Copy the spider diagram onto a large sheet of paper.
b) Complete each section with details about yourself.
c) Add extra areas if there are aspects of yourself that are missing.

This is me!
- Personality
- Name or nickname
- Dreams for the future
- Skills
- Secret talents
- Greatest achievement
- Heroes
- Best experience
- Things to improve
- Favourite item
- Interests
- Dislikes
- Best qualities

A person specification

A person specification is usually drawn up when an employer is preparing a job advertisement. A job description outlines the main duties of the job, while the person specification defines the qualities, skills, attitudes, knowledge and experience that are necessary or useful to do a specific job. Some things will be identified as 'essential' for the job while others will be 'desirable' – an added bonus. When an employer receives application forms they match them against the person specification in order to draw up a shortlist of candidates to interview. Those applicants that meet all the essential criteria could form the shortlist. However, if there are too many possible candidates, then the desirable criteria will be applied.

Activity 3 Could this be me?

Individually:
a) Read the person specifications for the three different jobs on the right and choose one job to apply for.

- Consider each job in turn and decide which best matches your personal profile.
- Rate your suitability for each job from 1 to 5, where 1 is not a good match and 5 is an excellent match.
- Give reasons for your views.

In pairs:
b) Interview your partner for the job for which they think they are most suited. Ask questions based on the person specification.

- How well can your partner present their skills and qualities?
- Would you hire your partner for the job?
- Explain your reasons and suggest any skills you think your partner needs to develop.

JOBS

RECEPTIONIST

Essential
Strong interpersonal skills
Excellent oral and written communication skills
Good organisational skills
Good ICT skills
Confident and friendly
Able to prioritise workload
Able to use initiative in dealing with the unexpected
Enjoy meeting and dealing with a variety of people

Desirable
Able to speak a foreign language

LANDSCAPE ARCHITECT

Essential
Design and drawing skills
Physically fit
Practical approach to work
Good oral communication
Good ICT skills
Knowledge of plants and their care
Able to negotiate
Able to work alone or in a team
Good financial skills

Desirable
Be able to drive

SOUND TECHNICIAN

Essential
An interest and appreciation of music
An ear for good quality sound
Be highly motivated
Good technical understanding of sound equipment
Have stamina and can cope with long unsociable hours
Good communication skills
Able to explain technical problems
Able to work under pressure

Desirable
Good head for heights
Musical ability

Education for Employability

39 CAN I WORK IN EUROPE?

Learning intentions

I am learning:
- ✓ which countries form the European Union (EU)
- ✓ why the EU was formed
- ✓ to evaluate the option of working in another EU country.

The European Union (EU) is made up of 27 countries that have formed a partnership with each other. Its aim is 'Peace, prosperity and freedom for its 495 million citizens – in a fairer, safer world'.

The EU was originally formed after the Second World War with six countries working together: France, Belgium, the Netherlands, Luxembourg, Italy and West Germany. Many more countries including the UK and Ireland have since joined (see below for a list of the current members).

Austria
Belgium
Bulgaria
Cyprus
Czech Republic
Denmark
Estonia
Finland
France
Germany
Greece
Hungary
Ireland

Italy
Latvia
Lithuania
Luxembourg
Malta
Netherlands
Poland
Portugal
Romania
Slovakia
Slovenia
Spain
Sweden
United Kingdom

Activity 1 Fly the flag

Individually:

a) Choose one of the EU countries to research (www.europa.eu/abc/european_countries is a useful website). Find out:

- when the country joined the EU
- its population
- the language(s) spoken
- one more interesting fact.

b) Make a copy of the flag of your chosen country and write all of your information below the flag.

As a class:

c) Display a map of Europe on the wall and use string to link all your flags and facts to each country in the EU.

One of the benefits of being in the EU is that it gives us all much more freedom to travel and work in different countries. People choose to move abroad for lots of different reasons like the ones on the opposite page.

To have a better quality of life

To take advantage of lower house prices and a higher standard of living

To live in a country with a better climate

Better job opportunities

To obtain a better life–work balance

To provide a better education for their children

To be with someone they love

To experience different cultures

To enjoy a more relaxing, laid-back way of life

Activity 2 Moving to Northern Ireland

Meet the Vadisova Family. They have decided to leave their home in Estonia to move to Northern Ireland.

In groups:
a) Prepare a presentation or brochure to encourage the Vadisova family to come and live in your local area.
b) Think about what will be important to them and organise your information under useful headings.
c) The children will need schools and the parents will need jobs; they may be concerned about housing and other amenities such as hospitals and leisure facilities, transport, and shops.
d) Check out your local council website for help.

Changes in technology also mean that it is much easier for people who move to another country to keep in touch with family and friends back home. This has encouraged many people who may not have considered emigrating a few years ago to take the plunge. However, there are still more people arriving in Northern Ireland than leaving. What will you do?

Activity 3 To move or not to move

In groups:
a) List all the reasons you can think of as to why people do not leave Northern Ireland to move abroad.

Individually:
b) Compare the reasons for moving from above to the reasons for staying in your list to weigh up which are most important to you.

- Draw a diagram of some scales. Label the two sides 'Stay' and 'Go'.
- Add reasons that are important to you on the appropriate side.
- Which side wins? 'Stay' or 'Go'?

Education for Employability

40 WHERE IN THE WORLD CAN I WORK?

Learning intentions

I am learning:
- ✓ about different opportunities for a gap year
- ✓ about the benefits of a gap year
- ✓ what skills I need to work in other countries around the world.

In the last topic you learned how being a part of the EU makes it a lot easier for people to travel and work in Europe. An increase in airlines and more flight destinations also make travelling and working in other countries around the world much more accessible. There are opportunities for young people to emigrate permanently or work abroad for a short time during a gap year before starting work or further education.

A gap year can be used to spend time travelling, to develop new skills through further study, or to gain work experience. You can do voluntary work or get a paid job. Read about two students and what they did below.

Ellie Messham volunteered with Students Partnership Worldwide (SPW) in Uganda

I wanted to work with an organisation that didn't just teach English or build wells. I wanted to work with people and really get to know a country and its culture. I was looking for an organisation that was really going to make a difference, work with local people and to know that what I did would be sustained after I left the project. I chose to volunteer with SPW.

After a month of training in Uganda, I spent eight months living in a rural village, Bulopa, raising awareness of HIV/AIDS amongst young people. Julius, my Ugandan counterpart, and I worked mainly in the primary school. The highlight of my placement was organising a Health Festival. It involved dramas, dances and songs, all based on HIV prevention or living positively with AIDS, performed by our students, Non-Governmental Organisations (NGOs) and the much loved Ugandan tradition of speeches. The best part was that the AIDS Information Centre (AIC) came to our village and offered free HIV tests. I remember vividly how excited the deputy head of my school was when he found out he was HIV negative.

My time in Uganda has stayed with me in the UK. It has given me a new, more global perspective on life. Volunteering allowed me to test myself, to see what I could do. I would recommend volunteering overseas to everyone; you will get more out of it than you put in without question!

www.spw.org

Lucy Feltham worked on an outback ranch in Australia with Real Gap Experience

I emerged from my Outback Ranch Training week with all the skills of a fully fledged cowgirl and was looking forward to starting my work placement. My placement was at a cattle station called Flora Valley. The property is 33,000 square kilometres and has 35,000 head of Brahman cattle. I was the only girl amongst 15 cowboys, which was a bit daunting! I had a room with a bed and a wooden shelf in it along with loads of lizards and goodness knows what else.

My time at the station was the best of my life. I worked there for just over three months. I spent most days out mustering where we would take out around five horses and a couple of motorbikes and walk, on average, 1500 cattle for about 20 km a time. Whilst walking the cattle we would sing and play games to entertain ourselves. The rest of the time would be yard work which involved branding and castrating the calves and processing, injecting and trucking the cattle.

On our days off we would either go to the creek and have a swim with the 'freshies' and a BBQ or bring in some Mickey bulls and ride them in the yards with buck straps and chaps – proper rodeo style!

All in all my time at Flora was fantastic. It was VERY hard work, we worked from 5 a.m. to 8 p.m., six or seven days a week and the heat (40 degrees plus!) was hard to cope with at first. It was definitely worth it; I couldn't have asked for anything better from my experience.

www.realgap.co.uk

Activity 1 Taking a year out

In pairs:
a) Use one of the websites from the case studies on page 80 or research the internet to find the story of a gap year student.
b) Consider their experiences. What skills do you think they developed?
c) Prepare a presentation to explain the benefits of this gap year to share with the class.

Although there are many opportunities to work abroad for a short period of time, if you wish to migrate to another country permanently it can be more difficult to gain access. For countries like the USA, Canada, New Zealand or Australia you need to qualify for a visa and sometimes pass a points test. For instance, for Australian immigration, you usually need to gain 120 points. Points are awarded for various reasons including skills, age, the job you are trained for, what level you are qualified to, how much experience you have, whether your occupation is in demand, and whether you already have a job offer.

Activity 2 The awesome Aussie

In pairs:
a) Research the requirements to qualify for an Australian working visa. The website www.visabureau.com/australia/working-holiday-visa.aspx may help you.
b) Find examples of jobs that are in demand in Australia.
c) Design an 'awesome Australian applicant'. Write a brief description of them, including the skills and attributes that would help them obtain a visa.

> Taking a gap year is now widely approved by both employers and universities as students develop many valuable skills and qualities. Students are often more mature, experienced, independent and hard-working after a gap year and therefore more likely to succeed in future jobs and courses.

Age	Points
18–29	30
30–34	25
35–39	20
40–44	15

Australian immigration points for age

Activity 3 Personal journal

- Would you consider living in another country? Why or why not?
- If so, what are the implications for any career plans you are forming?

Education for Employability

41 CAN I MAKE A DIFFERENCE BY WORKING IN BUSINESS?

Learning intentions

I am learning:
- how businesses and organisations can contribute to the local community
- why businesses want to make a difference in the community
- how local businesses could contribute to our school community.

When businesses operate in your local area they provide the local community with jobs and services. But what other differences do they make? What do they do to help in your local area? Many large employers such as supermarkets have voucher schemes to provide equipment for schools. These voucher schemes are very well-known examples of how businesses contribute to the local community.

An example of vouchers for schools

Other companies (both large and small) also make valuable contributions. Below are two examples of how companies are making a difference in their communities.

Adopt a school is teaching all a valuable lesson

St Matthew's Primary School has developed a close working relationship with PricewaterhouseCoopers, a large global accountancy firm with offices in Belfast. Volunteers from PricewaterhouseCoopers come into school and help pupils with their ICT, reading and maths skills. They also help parents with further studies and advise the school about their finances.
With the 'Adopt a school' project PricewaterhouseCoopers are helping the school, the children and their parents.

Belfast Telegraph 24 April 2007

Supervalu helps charity get BIG BUS on the road

Supervalu, the supermarket chain, has helped Action Cancer get a £1.5 million mobile unit on the road. The BIG BUS was launched by Gloria Hunniford, the TV presenter, whose daughter Caron Keating died from breast cancer. Services on the BIG BUS include digital breast screening, health promotion and men's health checks. Action Cancer Chief Executive Robin McRoberts said 'We are very excited to unveil the BIG BUS and to get it on the road … SuperValu are funding over £600,000 of the cost. We are very grateful to them for their invaluable support.' Action Cancer says the new service will help thousands of people annually by reaching right into the heart of communities.

www.bitc.org.uk

Education for Employability

Activity 1 Making a difference

a) As a class brainstorm other examples of businesses making a difference in your community. They may be in your school, youth group, or the area you live in. What conclusions can you draw from this?
b) Read the two case studies on page 82. The benefits to the local community are obvious, but as a class discuss why these companies bother with these activities.
c) Is working for a company where you can make a difference important to you? Why?

We have looked at just a few ways in which companies can make a contribution to their local communities, but there are many other innovative ways of doing this.

Activity 2 Who does what?

In groups:
a) Find out about a local organisation and what it contributes to its community. You could research using the following:

- the internet – www.bitc.org.uk is a good starting point
- the local newspaper
- by writing to local companies asking them what they do or looking at their websites for information
- by inviting someone from a local employer into school to tell you what they are doing.

b) Present your findings to the rest of the class. Explain what is being done and how you think it benefits the community and the company.

Activity 3 Ask and receive

In groups:
a) Think up one simple scheme or activity in which you could involve a local company that would benefit your class or school community.
b) Decide on the company.
c) Put your suggestion to the rest of the class and agree on the best scheme.
d) Plan how you could approach the firm you have chosen.
e) Approach the firm with your idea.

Education for Employability

42 CAN I WORK FOR MYSELF?

Learning intentions

I am learning:
- ✓ about how ideas for new businesses are generated
- ✓ to understand some of the steps for setting up a new business.

One option you have when you leave full-time education is to choose to work for yourself. Some people find that they gain greater job satisfaction through being their own boss rather than working for someone else. However, it is not an easy option. Anyone starting up a business needs both a good idea and a lot of luck.

Businesses are generally based on the making and selling of products, or the provision of services. Ideas for new businesses can emerge in a range of ways, for example:

- You wanted to buy something locally but couldn't find it, so you decide there is a need worth exploring.
- You enjoy an unusual sport or hobby and realise others might be interested in getting involved too.
- You decide to make best use of a particular skill or talent you have such as performing magic tricks at children's parties.

One common approach to creating a business idea is to select a 'target group' and imagine what their lives are like to identify services or products they might wish to buy. For example, consider the home, family, leisure and work life of a working mother. If you think through the types of things she does each day, you will realise how busy her lifestyle is, so there are many things she might want to make her life easier. See hexagon for examples.

Products: Prepacked school lunches, Washing and ironing, Convenience foods, Party organising, House cleaning, Home hairdressing, Child care, Dog walking, Disposable nappies

Lifestyle: Busy

Target group: Working mothers

Services: Personal training

💡 Activity 1 Finding the right idea

In groups:
a) Copy the hexagon diagram above onto a large sheet of paper.
b) Select a 'target group' (such as teenage girls, toddlers, retired people, primary-school-aged boys) and write it in the centre.
c) Discuss key aspects of their lifestyle and add them to the diagram.
d) For each lifestyle aspect, write down products that you think the target group would be interested in buying.

e) Repeat for any services you think they may be interested in.
f) Could any of these ideas be developed into a new business idea?

- Consider all the ideas and decide which are the most unusual or original.
- Make a shortlist, then pick the one that you think could be turned into a real business.

After you have an idea for a business, you need to write a business plan. A business plan is a document prepared when a business is being set up for the first time in order to show potential investors that the company is worth investing in.

Activity 2 Developing a business plan

In groups:
Based on the product or service your group has selected draw up a business plan. Copy and complete the business plan template below including as much information as you can. Use the questions to help you.

Business plan
Business name
What will your business be called?
Business idea
What is the product or service? *Why has this the potential to be successful?* *What competition will there be from others?* *How will the product/service be promoted?* *What will you charge?*
Target market
Whom is the product/service aimed at? *Why are these customers likely to buy it?*
Finance
What will you need money for? *Where might you get this money?*

Activity 3 Promoting your idea

Once you start your business, you will need to promote it to tell potential customers about your products or services.

In groups:
a) Decide whether to use advertising or the press to promote your business or product.

In pairs:
b) Create one of the following promotional items:

- Design an advert or flier
- Write a headline with a short news story to appear in a newspaper.

c) As a group select the best one to present to the rest of the class.

Education for Employability

43 COULD I START A BUSINESS?

Learning intentions

I am learning:
- ✓ to recognise entrepreneurial characteristics
- ✓ to identify some of the key actions taken by entrepreneurs in achieving their goals
- ✓ to understand if I already have what it takes to be an entrepreneur.

Previously we have looked at the possibility of starting a business. Now we are going to focus on what makes a successful entrepreneur, and the types of experiences they have to deal with if they wish to take a business idea and turn it into a reality.

Sir Alan Sugar

An entrepreneur is someone who has a good idea and turns it into a successful business. Research has shown that there are certain qualities and attitudes – 'characteristics' – commonly found amongst successful business people. These have been described as a 'can do' attitude. A typical entrepreneur will have the following key characteristics.

Characteristic	Self-starter	Self-confidence	Self-determination	Perseverance	Initiative	Commitment	Judgement
Definition	The ability to take the initiative, work independently and to develop your ideas	A self-belief and passion about your business – your enthusiasm should win people over to your ideas	A belief that the outcome of events is down to your own actions, rather than based on external factors or other people's actions	The ability to continue despite setbacks, financial insecurity and exposure to risk	The ability to be resourceful and proactive, rather than adopting a passive 'wait and see' approach	The willingness to make personal sacrifices through long hours and loss of leisure time	The ability to be open-minded when listening to other people's advice, while bearing in mind your objectives for the business

Based on the entrepreneurial quality check www.nibusinessinfo.co.uk

Activity 1 Pia the entrepreneur

Read the interview with Pia on the opposite page. Identify when she demonstrated any of the entrepreneurial characteristics above. Create a table to list each characteristic in the left-hand column and an example of how Pia demonstrated that characteristic in the right-hand column.

Education for Employability

86

PIA'S PIZZAS

Entrepreneur interview
Name: Pia
Business: Pia's Pizzas
Industry: Hospitality and catering

Why did you choose to open a pizza restaurant?
I had always loved cooking. My family were originally from Italy and I had been making pizza and other Italian specialities since I was a young girl. When my children started secondary school I felt the time was right to go back to work.

I identified a gap in the market. It's hard to believe but back in the 1980s in Northern Ireland there were very few pizza restaurants. Due to 'the troubles' there were very few restaurants and almost no pizza places. I guess I recognised a market at the right time.

What did you do to turn your idea into a business?
The first thing I did was to go and talk to people I knew who ran their own businesses to find out the realities of working for yourself … although many tried, I was not put off. I just had a gut feeling that I could do this!

The next thing was to raise money for the rent of premises and to allow the fitting of a specialist pizza oven. I took a big risk at the time … I begged, borrowed money from my family and friends. I had been turned down by the bank.

I began to search for premises in the centre of the town. I was lucky I found a restaurant which had recently closed so it was well kitted out. I then went about hiring staff.

Later I drew up a business plan … this allowed me to get a bank loan.

What problems did you encounter during the creation of your business and how did you deal with them?
Things did not always go smoothly. I faced a range of teething problems with staff, the new oven … the night before we opened I did not sleep.

It was difficult to build up custom at first. Word of mouth was very important for attracting customers. I worked very hard to make people feel welcome so that not only would they return but they would tell others.

I also worked to attract young people by keeping prices low. I did a lot of marketing for the first two years to get established, trading on the novelty value of being the only pizza restaurant in town. But there were times when I did not know how I was going to pay the bills or the staff wages. It was sheer single-minded determination and belief that I would succeed that kept me going. I would not have survived those early years without my very supportive family.

Who did you use for help and guidance during the start-up of the business?
I found a 'silent partner' who was willing to invest in the business but leave me to develop it as I wished.

They had experience in the catering trade and were able to point me in the right direction. I got some funding to train staff from the Northern Ireland Catering Industry Training Board. I also got a grant from the Chamber of Commerce (today it would be Invest Northern Ireland) to go to the USA and study how pizza restaurants had developed for the mass market.

Do you have a growth strategy for the business?
I am continually looking to develop new markets reaching out to different sectors. For example, dining aimed specifically at families; early bird menus which attract students; catering for parties and events which has taken off recently. However, home deliveries are still the mainstay of the business.

Do you have any regrets?
Some. Not so much for myself but for my family and my children, who I feel have missed out. I had to work very long hours at the beginning. When I wasn't in the restaurant I was at the wholesalers buying stock or in the office doing accounts. We did not have a family holiday for years.

But now life is great. I make a very good living and enjoy life to the full. I have excellent staff working for me who take a lot of the pressure and I have an accountant to look after the books. I can take holidays whenever I want, I have a second home in France and I change my car each year … I really am very lucky.

Education for Employability

43 COULD I START A BUSINESS? CONTINUED

Activity 2 What makes it work?

Pia was determined to start her own business and nothing, it seems, would stop her. Starting up a business requires a considerable investment of time, funds and energy.

Individually:

a) From Pia's interview on page 87 draw up the following lists:

- some of the things she had to do to start her own business
- some of the difficulties she faced
- the reasons behind starting her own business
- some reasons for her success.

In pairs:

b) Share your lists with a partner and combine them to create one long list.

c) Select items from your lists that you feel are either the *rewards* or *demands* of starting your own business.

Examples of the rewards and demands of running your own business

Activity 3 Do you have what it takes?

Perhaps you will consider starting you own business when you are older. But have you got what it takes? Here is an opportunity to assess whether you might be a budding entrepreneur. Test yourself by answering the questions on the next page to find out.

a) Read each statement in turn. Does it apply to you always, sometimes or never? Make a note of your answer.

b) When you have the finished the quiz, rate yourself:

- Score 2 points for every 'always' answer.
- Score 1 point for every 'sometimes' answer.
- Score 0 points for every 'never' answer.

c) Find your total score by adding the points together. Check the scoring to find out your entrepreneurial potential!

ENTREPRENEURIAL QUIZ

Statement	Always	Sometimes	Never
I am prepared to work very hard to my achieve my goals.			
I cope with uncertainty well.			
I have a positive attitude to life.			
I am always prepared to take a chance.			
I am not afraid to take risks.			
I know whether I will be able to do something.			
I bounce back from setbacks.			
I can trust others to do things for me.			
I like making money.			
I learn new things quickly.			
I am willing to ask for help when I need it.			
I am happy to take advice from experts.			
I am happy to work on my own.			
I like to be in charge.			
If I want something I will get it.			
I enjoy trying new things.			
I like to do things my way.			
I like new challenges.			
I can stay motivated for long periods.			
I like to think up new ideas.			
I am competitive and like to win.			
Total scores			

Scoring

If you scored:

- between 42 and 28, you are an entrepreneur in the making!
- between 27 and 14, you could be an entrepreneur.
- less than 14, perhaps being an entrepreneur is not for you?

Very few entrepreneurs can claim to be strong in all of the areas required. The key is to make the most of your strengths and take action to address any gaps in your skills. This could include learning new skills yourself or drawing on others to help you build a business. In the end, you are the only person who can decide whether you have what it takes to start a real business!

Activity 4
Personal journal

a) What have I learned about my entrepreneurial skills?
b) Is self-employment a future option for me?
c) Which subjects should I study if I want to start my own business?

Education for Employability

ANSWERS

Answers to Topic 17, Activity 1

A Article 20
B Article 18
C Article 19
D Article 21

Answers to Topic 22, Activity 1

1 The local council is responsible for examples 1, 3, 6, 10.
2 The Northern Ireland Assembly is responsible for examples 4, 7, 9.
4 The House of Commons is responsible for 2, 8.
5 The European Parliament is responsible for 5.

Answers to Topic 27, Activity 2

1 Criminal law examples: 1, 2, 4, 5, 8, 9.
2 Civil law examples: 3, 6, 7, 10.

Answers to Topic 29, Activity 1

A 4
B 5
C 6
D 3
E 2
F 1

INDEX

A
Action Cancer 82
action planning cycle 10
action plans 10–11
action projects 48–49
'Adopt a school' project 82
Afghanistan 52
alcohol 20–21
Aung San Suu Kyi 50
Australia 80, 81

B
BIG BUS 82
birth control 26–27
Bloom, Benjamin 12
Buddhists 52
Burma 50
business plans 85
businesses
  in local communities 82–83
  starting up new 84–89

C
careers
  choosing 66–67
  developing employability skills 76
  in demand 72–73
  matching essential skills with 70–71
  matching motivational factors to 74–75
  person specifications for 77
careers advice 65
change, managing 18–19
Children's Law Centre 55
children's rights 36–37
CID 65, 67
citizen participation 32–33, 34–35
citizenship 60–61
civil law 54–55
communities
  affect of crime on 56–57
  business contributions to the local 82–83
  finding help in 30–31
  participation in 40–41
  taking democratic action in 46–49
concept maps 33
condoms 26, 29
Confederation of British Industry (CBI) 76
contraception 26–27

crime
  and affect on the community 56–57
  bringing criminals to justice 58–59
  reasons for committing 57
Criminal Justice System 58
criminal law 54–55
critical thinking 12–13

D
Dalai Lama 52
decision-making 62–63
  by political representatives 44–45
democracy
  characteristics of 50–51
  citizen participation 32–33
  decision-making in a 44–45
  laws in a 54–55
  meaning of 32
  political representation 42–43, 44–45
  role of human rights 52–53
  taking action in a 46–49
depression 31
'devolved Assembly' 43
DiClemente, Carlo 18
double standards 2

E
emigration 79, 81
employability skills 76
employment trends 72
entrepreneurs 86–89
  characteristics of 86
  entrepreneurial quiz 88–89
  interview 87
Europe, working in 78–79
European Parliament 42, 44–45
European Union (EU) 78
external motivation 16

F
female, being 22–23
firefighters 73

G
Gandhi, Mohandas (Mahatma) 50
gap year 80–81
GCSEs
  discovering the 'options' 68–69
  goal of choosing 63
  help with choosing 64–65
  and motivation 16

  preferred learning styles and environments 68–69
  subjects for essential skills 70–71
  and thinking about a career 66–67
gender 22–23
gender identity 22
gender stereotyping 22–23

H
'Handy Refusal Skills' 14
Hawkins, David 14
Health Promotion Agency 28
help, finding 30–31
House of Commons 42, 44–45
human rights
  absolute 53
  abuses of 51, 52
  participation 34–35
  role in a democracy 52–53

I
'I AM' risk management 20
identity, gender 22
immigration, Australian 81
impulses 8–9
India 50
integrity 2–3
internal motivation 16
international human rights law 52–53
interviewing
  an entrepreneur 87
  workers 72–73

J
job descriptions 77
job profiles 73
job satisfaction 74–75
jobs in demand 72–73

L
landscape architects 77
laws
  affects of breaking 56–57
  in a democracy 54–55
  enforcing 58–59
  international human rights 52–53
learning environments 69
learning styles 68–69
local council 42, 44–45
loneliness 24–25
Lundy, Dr Laura 36

M

male, being 22–23
Maslow's pyramid of need 74
media 51
Mooney, Anna 86
motivation 16–17, 76
   Maslow's pyramid of need 74
   in work 74–75
motivational factors 74–75
moving abroad 78–79, 80–81

N

non-democratic societies 50–51, 52
Northern Ireland Assembly 42–43, 44–45

O

Odyssey 65, 67
Oxfam 46

P

Parks, Rosa 50
participation
   children's rights of 36–37
   in the community 40–41
   in a democracy 32–33
   as a human right 34–35
   in school 38–39
Pathfinder 65, 67
peer pressure 14
person specifications 77
personal change 18–19
personal profiles 77
personal responsibility 6–7
Pia's Pizza 87
planning 10–11
Pol Pot 51
political institutions 42–43
   decision-making in 44–45
political protests 50–51
problem solving 12–13
Prochaska, James 18
protests, political 50–51

Q

questionnaires, job 72–73

R

Real Gap Experience 80
receptionists 77
refusal skills 14–15
representatives, political 42–43, 44–45
responsibility, personal 6–7
risk management for alcohol 20

S

schools
   'Adopt a school' project 82
   participation in 38–39
   voucher schemes for 82
self-control 8–9, 14
self-employment 84–89
self-motivation 16–17
sexually transmitted infections (STIs) 26, 28–29
skills
   developing employability 76
   for work 70–71
   for working abroad 81
smoking 30
society, participation in 40–41
sound technicians 77
South Africa 52
spiritual assets 4
spiritual worldview 4–5
spirituality 4
'Stages of Change model' 18–19
stereotyping, gender 22–23
STIs (sexually transmitted infections) 26, 28–29
Students Partnership Worldwide (SPW) 80
supermarkets 82

T

target groups 84–85

U

Uganda 80
United Nations Convention on the Rights of the Child (UNCRC) 36–37, 52
United States of America 50
Universal Declaration of Human Rights (UDHR) 34–35, 52

V

volunteering overseas 80
voucher schemes 82

W

work
   in another EU country 78–79
   developing employability skills 76
   interviewing people in different sectors 72–73
   job satisfaction 74–75
   overseas 78–79, 80–81
   skills for 70–71
   starting up a new business 84–89
   voluntary 80
worldviews 4–5